$aving Money with the Tightwad Twins

More Than 1,000 Practical Tips for Women on a Budget

... Plus 5 Really BIG Tips That Can Change Your Financial Life Today!

Ann & Susan Fox
with Charlotte Fox Messmer
Illustrations by Nathan W. Vaughn

Health Communications, Inc.
Deerfield Beach, Florida

www.hcibooks.com

Library of Congress Cataloging-in-Publication Data

Fox, Ann
    Saving money with the tightwad twins : 1,000 practical tips for women on a budget — plus 5 really big tips that can change your financial life today / Ann Fox Chodakowski, Susan Fox Wood with Charlotte Fox Messmer ; illustrations by Nathan W. Vaughn.
    p. cm.
    ISBN 0-7573-0105-3 (tp)
    1. Finance, Personal. 2. Saving and investment. I. Fox, Susan, 1952–
II. Messmer, Charlotte Fox. III. Title.
HG179.F668 2003
332.024/042—dc21   2003047875

©2003 Ann Fox and Susan Fox
ISBN 0-7573-0105-3

Publisher: Health Communications, Inc.
              3201 S.W. 15th Street
              Deerfield Beach, FL 33442-8190

Cover design and illustrations by Larissa Hise Henoch
Inside book design by Lawna Patterson Oldfield

This book is dedicated to "the forgotten woman." Not everyone knows her. Only the women who have been in her shoes will recognize her. Most men do not. Please observe the illustration of her on page vii. It is self-explanatory. But for those of you who do not know her, then, we offer this description:

> She is the mother who nearly froze to death sitting on metal gym seats at the football games every Friday night instead of watching from her car so that when her children asked, "Did you see me?" she could say, "Of course!"
>
> She is the mother who sat up nights with a sick toddler in her arms, wiping up throw-up of hot dogs and cherry Kool-Aid and went to work the next day.
>
> She is the mother who has a full-time job at home or at work or both and awakens early each day, all the while knowing her job will never end and will probably be much the same as yesterday.
>
> She is the mother who can nurse a baby, sew on a button and monitor homework all at the same time.
>
> She is the mother who tries to help with the budget, alone or together with a mate, but still comes up short every month.
>
> She is the mother who gets her hair and nails done at the local beauty school and feels like a queen when she does.
>
> She is the mother who reads the same bedtime story twice a night for over a year and who teaches her children their alphabet

and how to tie their shoelaces before they start school so they won't be behind the other children.

She is the mother who watches the news reports about the stock market but is really worrying about the washing machine repair bill due tomorrow and how much she has left from the budget to buy groceries.

She is the mother who laughs when the magazines do a story on inexpensive clothing for only $125 per dress, remembering how she broke out in a cold sweat the day she bought a dress to go to a wedding for $32.95.

She is the mother who passes by the name-brand clothes and groceries, knowing she can whip up something just as good or better without paying for a name.

She is the mother who may have lost her own mother but carries on bravely, just as her mother would expect her to do.

She is the mother who has had to maneuver bills like the Indy 500.

She is the mother who always has time for her family but never enough time for herself.

The Tightwad Twins salute her and dedicate this book to her.

The Forgotten Woman . . .

We dedicate this book to her!

Contents

PART THREE:
Turning Trash into Cash: Million-Dollar Tips That Will Change Your Financial Life Forever

PART FOUR:
The Silver Lining: Testimonials from Our Fans Say These Tips Really Work!

Introduction

Let's get right to the point: We are cheap. We have had to be. We have survived and even thrived on a tight budget for most of our lives. Having helped many families survive financially over the years through our tips, we decided to write our biggest and most informative tip book yet.

Now let's get to another point. I am Ann, and I am the bossier twin. Therefore, I will tell you about our target. She is the *forgotten woman*. While other financial books are giving advice about money markets, we are giving advice to help the struggling woman on a really, really, really tight budget! She is forgotten, this woman of little time and no dime as our sister, Charlotte, would say. Our target is the woman who rushes to work with a toddler hanging from her legs only to rush back again after work to a hungry family; stacks of homework to supervise; laundry mounds the size of Texas; grocery and errand lists a mile long; bills, bills, and more bills; plus, home repairs all in between and squeezing her paycheck to death. She is worried about making the house payment or rent or how she will pay for the next repair on her car. She may be single or she may be married, working or a stay-at-home mom.

However, the problems are always the same: not enough time or money. This is where our mission comes in.

Our mission is simple. It is to *eliminate* the biggest bills of your budget or at least *reduce* them drastically, as well as show you how to manage your time and organize your home more efficiently through shortcuts that we have tested for years *so that your life can be drastically changed for the better.* You will not read about mutual funds or 401k plans in this book. As a matter of fact, this book is not for everyone. Some people will think this book is absurd—those who have not been poor enough. But for those of you who actually "get us," this book will be a gold mine.

Many of you know from previous books that we grew up in a tightwad family with a tightwad mother and father and had a big sister and a big brother. Our mother died when we were twenty-one, but her tightwad advice lingers on. Our father, also a pretty good tightwad in his own right, is now eight-six and was a master of trash-to-treasure when we were children. You will read about some of their tightwad tips throughout the book. And now for *"our"* story.

Susan and I were talking on the phone in 1995, and we happened to discuss something ridiculous: "Let's call ourselves the Tightwad Twins and go on television with an 800-number on our cheap green shirts and sell our mail-order tip book!" And that is what we did. Our family thought we were nuts or at least nuttier than usual. We just realized that we have only three talents: We are twins, we are tightwads and we are good at talking! However, we were not discouraged and ignored our critics and compiled all of our tips, which we put in a spiral-bound book. Then we were guests on the *Maury Povich Show* and displayed some of our trash-to-treasure items, chased Maury around a bit with his wastebasket, and the rest is history. We got 70,000 orders the week the show aired! Needless to say, we were overwhelmed, because we did all of the work ourselves and were soon looking for an agent to help get our book published so that we could rest a bit! Our first book, *Living on a Shoestring,* was published by Doubleday (we just knew this was a sign from God. . . . Doubleday . . . twins . . . get it?) Later, we had two more books published by Harvest House, *Moms Saving Money* and *101 Ways to Stretch Your Dollars.* We have had the privilege of appearing on numerous television and radio shows, as well being featured in quite a few well-known magazines such as *Family Circle* and many large newspapers. Our big sister, Charlotte, coauthored our first book with us and my adult son, Nathan, illustrated all of our, shall we say, "unusual" tightwad humor. We have been married, divorced and married again and have raised children in between. Needless to say, we understand the plight of the forgotten woman well . . . too well.

This is our favorite of all of our books because it focuses not only on our many smaller tips but also on the *bigger, life-changing ones.* We get such a thrill whenever we get an e-mail from a reader who used the "make money while you sleep" tip and changed his or her financial life forever. We hope you laugh with us as we share some humor only a woman could understand, as well as cry with us as we tell some of the inspirational tales sent to us by our readers over the years. Okay, tightwadettes, get ready to get serious about changing your financial plight! As our mama and daddy used to say, *"You never know the value of water until your well runs dry."*

Well, our wells have been dry . . . if yours has, too, then read on.

—*Tightwad Twin Ann,* the smarter twin

This is a picture of our beautiful sister, Charlotte (far left), who helped us write our first book. We are including all of her tips from that book in this book . . . she adds "class to our trash."

This photo is us with our brother Jim. He looks harmless here.

A Tightwad Tale

Once upon a time in 1952, identical twin babies were born. They grew up in a loving home with a big sister and a big brother, a hardworking father and a mother who raised them on a tightwad budget.

Because this family lived on a very, very small budget, the twins grew up knowing the value of a dollar. Later in their lives, they wrote down some of their tightwad tips and shared them with other women.

The twins were not fancy, nor did they have a fancy publisher. They did their mail-order manual all by themselves, and it was very hard. Noticed by two fancy publishers who loved them, the twins were very happy, knowing that their hard work had paid off and that they could share some of their tips with even more women.

The twins wrote more and more as time went on, appeared on big TV and radio shows, all the while knowing in their hearts that they had done their best and that not everyone would understand their tightwad ways. But that was okay because the twins wrote only for those who realized the value of "common cents" knowledge and how it can change your life.

And that's the truth.

*We are hereby tendering our
resignations as adults, effective immediately.
We have decided we want to be
eight years old again.*

PART ONE

ON THE HOME FRONT:
A Trash-Talkin' Primer for Making Your Humble Abode a Castle Fit for a Tightwad Queen

Cleaning on a Tightwad Budget

O ur mother always said that "Even if you are poor, soap is cheap and there is no excuse for being dirty!" We remembered that in our own homes and now offer to our readers some shortcuts when cleaning. So if you need some help in this area and agree with us that "cleaning" is actually a very "dirty" word, then read on.

Try these "recipes" for common household cleaning products that won't wipe away your budget:

- **All-purpose household cleaner:** ¹/₂ cup white vinegar, 1 cup ammonia, ¹/₄ cup baking soda, 1 gallon water.
- **Automatic dishwasher detergent:** Mix 1 cup borax and ¹/₂ cup baking soda with 3 cups of cheap automatic dishwasher detergent.
- **Cleanser for garbage disposals:** 1 cup baking soda, 1¹/₄ cups water. Mix ingredients and pour into ice cube trays and freeze. Turn on the disposal (no water running)

and dump about five to seven ice cubes down the drain, allowing the machine to grind them up.

- **Powdered carpet cleaner:** 2 cups baking soda, $\frac{1}{2}$ cup cornstarch, 1 tablespoon ground cloves. Sprinkle over the carpet, leave overnight and vacuum as usual.
- **Laundry pre-stain:** You can use a spray bottle for this one! Mix $\frac{1}{2}$ cup white vinegar, $\frac{1}{2}$ cup ammonia, $\frac{1}{2}$ cup of a store-bought liquid laundry soap and $\frac{1}{2}$ cup water. Spray stain, rub in mixture, let garment sit for a bit, then wash.
- **Stain remover for fabrics:** Mix $\frac{1}{2}$ cup dishwashing liquid, $\frac{1}{2}$ cup baking soda to 1 gallon of boiling water. Let your clothes soak in this overnight, then wash as you usually would.
- **Basic cleaner:** To 1 gallon of hot water, add 2 tablespoons baking soda and $\frac{1}{2}$ cup of detergent.
- **Furniture polish:** 1 part lemon juice and 2 parts vegetable oil. Polish as usual.
- **Toilet cleaner:** Use a 1 to 3 ratio of vinegar to water. Vinegar will remove many rust stains because it is a natural acid.
- **Glass cleaner:** Add 2 tablespoons cornstarch and $\frac{1}{2}$ cup white vinegar to 1 gallon of warm water.
- **Carpet deodorizer:** Baking soda. If it doesn't get the carpet smelling fresh, try a little more. Sprinkle a little then wait about seven to ten minutes and vacuum as usual.
- **Car wash mixture:** $\frac{1}{2}$ cup liquid detergent, $\frac{1}{3}$ cup baking soda, 1 gallon water. It only takes a cup of this solution in a bucket of warm water to wash a car.

Note: Label these homemade cleaners when you place them in spray bottles or regular bottles!

General Tips

- Store your steel wool scouring pads in the freezer and they won't rust.

- Save your soap slivers and put them in the microwave to melt. Pour this now-liquid soap into a dispenser or melt the soap in a smaller container and let it harden into a new bar of soap.

OUR TWO CENTS
Love It or Leave It

If you love something, set it free.
If it comes back, it will always be yours.
If it doesn't come back, it was
never yours to begin with
BUT,
If it just sits in your living room,
messes up your stuff,
eats all of your food, monopolizes
your phone, takes your money,
and doesn't seem to realize that you
are trying to set it free, then you
are either married to it
or gave birth to it.

- Instead of expensive air freshener, mix cheap liquid potpourri with water in a spray bottle. Spray on curtains, carpets, etc.

- A little perfume or cologne sprayed or dotted on a lightbulb will take the place of air fresheners.

- Sprinkle baking soda into your toilet once or twice a month and let it stand overnight.

- Reuse softener sheets by using spray potpourri on them.

- Used softener sheets also make great dust rags. Use them to clean your television and computer screen.

- Place pine needles in discreet places in the house, such as the bathroom, to rid a house of fleas.

- Two cups or so of white vinegar overnight in your toilet bowl makes any rings disappear.

- Fitted sheets and comforters really save time making the bed. Pin the bottom of the comforter with a huge diaper pin hidden under your comforter. When you make the bed, the comforter will be where you can just toss it back on!

OUR TWO CENTS
Did you ever wonder what would have happened if there were three wise women instead of three wise men? The women would have asked for directions, arrived on time, helped deliver the baby, cleaned the stable, made a casserole and brought disposable diapers as gifts!

- Clean out your car and purse on a set day of the week.
- When it comes to dishwashing detergents, you get more for your money by buying a name brand and using coupons.
- If you really must buy the cheapest dishwashing detergent, add 3 tablespoons of vinegar to the bottle to help cut grease on the dishes.
- Sand in a stand-up ashtray for inside or outside use is safer from fire, cleaner and more convenient for the smoker.
- Keep your fancier clothes clean with a dustcover made from an old pillowcase.

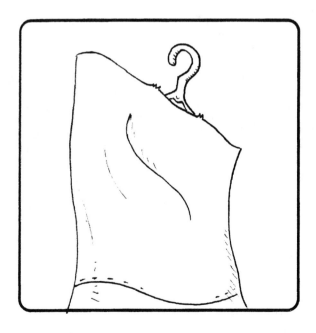

Pillowcase dust cover.

Use this list to keep your home clean and shiny. No household should be without it:

QUICK CLEANING

Living Room
☐ Clear clutter
☐ Clean glass, mirrors, tabletops
☐ Dust furniture, lamps, windowsills, pictures
☐ Empty wastebaskets
☐ Vacuum carpets, damp-mop floors

Bedrooms
☐ Clear clutter
☐ Straighten closet and hang up clothes
☐ Sort laundry for mending and dry cleaning
☐ Change linens
☐ Clean mirrors, glass, tabletops
☐ Dust furniture, windowsills, pictures
☐ Empty wastebaskets
☐ Vacuum or dust-mop floors/carpet

Bathrooms
☐ Clear clutter
☐ Collect dirty towels and take to laundry area
☐ Spray and wipe mirror with glass cleaner
☐ Clean sink
☐ Use glass cleaner on faucets and chrome
☐ Spray tub/shower walls with heavy-duty cleanser
☐ Squirt cleaner in toilet bowl and swish around bowl
☐ Wipe outside of bowl
☐ Wipe off windowsills

QUICK CLEANING *(continued)*

❏ Empty wastebaskets
❏ Vacuum carpets, damp-mop floor

Kitchen
❏ Organize clutter, including drawers
❏ Clean countertops
❏ Clean outside of large appliances with glass cleaner
❏ Shine outside of small appliances with glass cleaner
❏ Clean inside toaster oven, toaster and microwave
❏ Wipe off windowsills
❏ Wash and disinfect trash can, replace liner
❏ Sweet or vacuum floor, then damp-mop

Bigger Jobs: Rotate
❏ Polish wood furniture
❏ Use attachments to vacuum baseboards, moldings, lampshades and behind furniture
❏ Vacuum furniture and drapes
❏ Recycle magazines and newspapers
❏ Dust knickknacks, polish silver
❏ Clean inside cabinets and drawers
❏ Wash small rugs
❏ Scrub tile and grout
❏ Clean baseboards and woodwork
❏ Clean inside of medicine cabinet
❏ Wash shower curtain
❏ Scrub floor
❏ Clean range top thoroughly and replace burner bibs, vacuum vents
❏ Clean oven
❏ Clean woodwork
❏ Clean out pantry, cabinets and drawers
❏ Scrub and wax floor

YOU KNOW YOU'RE A TIGHTWAD . . .

. . . if you neglect to hear your name called in the doctor's office because you were busy looking in the trash bin for tossed magazines.

In the Kitchen

Our childhood kitchen with our mama cooking is a pleasant memory for us. Remember when mothers wore aprons and actually did sentry duty at the waffle iron? We do. Here are some time- and money-savers from our mother's kitchen to yours. (By the way, since we're in the kitchen section, it might be a good time to note that Ann weighs a full five pounds more than me. . . . She thinks gravy is a beverage).

For smart storage, recycle plastic peanut butter jars to store rice and other grains, beans and any dry goods that should be kept fresh and bug free. Since the jars are see-through, you don't have to label.

Cut up old terry-cloth towels and use them as dishrags or dish-drying towels.

Save paper bags and washed Styrofoam containers from fast-food places for your work lunches.

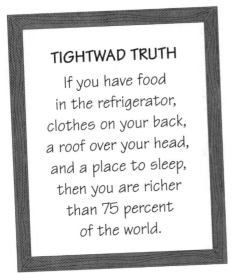

TIGHTWAD TRUTH

If you have food
in the refrigerator,
clothes on your back,
a roof over your head,
and a place to sleep,
then you are richer
than 75 percent
of the world.

Flat box tops make excellent stack trays for papers. Cut an end section out of one end of the box and stack it on top of another one.

Use the Styrofoam egg cartons for drawer organizers or for emergency ice trays.

Those chip clips are too easy to break. Use a rubber band and fold it around the entire bag of chips from the folded-down top to bottom.

Use cloth hair-set tape to label freezer items. It sticks and you can write on it.

Use your mustard squirt container for decorating icing designs on cakes.

Make a temporary cooler from a brown paper bag insulated with about an inch of folded newspaper.

Freeze water in a margarine tub. This makes a great punch bowl ice blob.

Save the plastic bowl-like bottoms of liter bottles. They make excellent containers for sponges and soaps.

Use the shower caps you get in hotels to cover bowls for microwave cooking or for your refrigerator.

Save cereal box liners to use as waxed paper. Use the liners for making pies and cookies.

Leave a stick of celery in the bread bag to keep it fresh.

Use your Crock-Pot and microwave to save on electricity. Plus your house does not heat up and dinner is done when you get home!

Nail an old bookshelf on the back of your kitchen or closet door. You now have the spice rack/pantry you have always wanted.

Keep your refrigerator full to make it cooler and more efficient. Use milk cartons or plastic jugs filled with water, if necessary.

You may save money by cooking from scratch, but if supper preparation stresses you out, then you need to look for the money-saving coupons for nutritional fast food.

Keep a tray or flat box in the refrigerator containing lunch items. This helps create assembly-line lunch-making.

If you can afford prepared or frozen foods and you work outside of the home, do it! Life is easier.

Do your weekly grocery shopping after you have cleaned your house and finished the laundry– your mind is more free for finding bargains.

> **OUR TWO CENTS**
> If at first you don't succeed, try reading the recipe!

THIS IS NOT ROCKET SCIENCE—SIMPLIFY YOUR LIFE WHENEVER YOU CAN! Keep a cute basket on the dining table filled with napkins, paper plates, forks and spoons, salt and pepper and so on. We call this "setting the table without really setting the table!"

Serve food from the stove top or kitchen counter in buffet fashion.

Label your refrigerator shelves LEFTOVERS, FRUIT, DRINKS, CONDIMENTS, etc. Knowing what you have or don't have helps making a grocery list so much easier, and saves you time and money in not buying duplicates of what you already have.

> **OUR TWO CENTS**
> Men love to barbeque.
> They will cook
> as long as there is
> danger involved.

Organize your refrigerator and cupboards to avoid buying duplicates and to avoid waste of leftovers.

SHOPPING LIST

Date _____

Staples
- ❏ Cereal
- ❏ Flour
- ❏ Jell-O
- ❏ Mixes
- ❏ Nuts
- ❏ Stuffing
- ❏ Sugar

Spices
- ❏ Bacon Bits
- ❏ Baking Powder
- ❏ Chocolate
- ❏ Coconut
- ❏ Salt/Pepper
- ❏ Soda

Pasta/Potatoes
- ❏ Instant Potatoes
- ❏ Mixes
- ❏ Pasta
- ❏ Rice
- ❏ Spaghetti

Drinks
- ❏ Apple Cider
- ❏ Coffee
- ❏ Sparkling Water
- ❏ Tea

Canned Goods/ Fresh Vegetables
- ❏ Canned Fruit
- ❏ Green Beans
- ❏ Carrots
- ❏ Corn
- ❏ Squash
- ❏ Dried Beans
- ❏ Pinto Beans
- ❏ Navy/White Beans
- ❏ Soups
- ❏ Tuna

Condiments
- ❏ Catsup
- ❏ Honey
- ❏ Jelly/Jam
- ❏ Mayonnaise

- ❏ Molasses
- ❏ Mustard
- ❏ Oil
- ❏ Peanut Butter
- ❏ Pickles
- ❏ Relish
- ❏ Salad Dressing
- ❏ Shortening
- ❏ Syrup
- ❏ Tomato Paste/ Sauce
- ❏ Vinegar

Paper Goods/Misc.
- ❏ Foil
- ❏ Napkins
- ❏ Paper Towels
- ❏ Plastic Wrap
- ❏ Tissues
- ❏ Toilet Tissue
- ❏ Toothpicks
- ❏ Trash Bags
- ❏ Waxed Paper
- ❏ Zip Bags

SHOPPING LIST *(continued)*

Household

- ❑ Bleach
- ❑ Clothes Detergent
- ❑ Dishwasher Detergent
- ❑ Dish Soap
- ❑ Pet Food
- ❑ Furniture Polish
- ❑ Lightbulbs
- ❑ Vacuum Bags
- ❑ Fabric Softener

Personal Items

- ❑ Body Soap
- ❑ Deodorant
- ❑ Feminine Products
- ❑ Hair Care
- ❑ Makeup
- ❑ Tooth Products

Frozen Food/Juice

- ❑ Ice Cream
- ❑ Juice
- ❑ TV Dinners

Pastry

- ❑ Bread/Buns
- ❑ Chips
- ❑ Cookies
- ❑ Crackers
- ❑ Croutons

Meat

- ❑ Beef
- ❑ Chicken
- ❑ Pizzas

Dairy Products

- ❑ Butter
- ❑ Milk
- ❑ Cottage Cheese
- ❑ Sour Cream
- ❑ Cheese

Other Products

- ❑ _____
- ❑ _____
- ❑ _____
- ❑ _____
- ❑ _____
- ❑ _____
- ❑ _____
- ❑ _____
- ❑ _____
- ❑ _____
- ❑ _____
- ❑ _____
- ❑ _____
- ❑ _____
- ❑ _____
- ❑ _____
- ❑ _____
- ❑ _____
- ❑ _____
- ❑ _____
- ❑ _____
- ❑ _____

NOTE: Make copies of this list and carry a copy with you each shopping trip!! Remember to always keep a master copy for future copying purposes.

MENU PLANNING
FOR THE WEEK OF _____

Include main meals, lunches, dinners, parties, extra events.

SUNDAY:

Breakfast _____

Lunch _____

Dinner _____

Other _____

MONDAY:

Breakfast _____

Lunch _____

Dinner _____

Other _____

TUESDAY:

Breakfast _____

Lunch _____

Dinner _____

Other _____

MENU PLANNING (continued)

WEDNESDAY:

Breakfast _____

Lunch _____

Dinner _____

Other _____

THURSDAY:

Breakfast _____

Lunch _____

Dinner _____

Other _____

FRIDAY:

Breakfast _____

Lunch _____

Dinner _____

Other _____

SATURDAY:

Breakfast _____

Lunch _____

Dinner _____

Other _____

SPECIAL OCCASIONS & EVENTS THIS WEEK:

Call _____

Do _____

Buy _____

YOU KNOW YOU'RE A TIGHTWAD . . .

. . . if the backyard squirrel is written on
your menu for next week's supper.

This is twin Susan. Let's get one thing straight. Ann can't cook. It's that simple. She hates it and, frankly, for our sakes, we are glad she does! Needless to say, I am the better cook, although our sister, Charlotte, is fabulous herself.

However, in this section, you will find only recipes that are truly "open the can or box, then dump, then lump." Three easy steps for the *really* rushed woman who lives in the real world—on a budget and always in a time crunch. Many of the recipes are adapted from food companies we all know and trust.

One thing of importance: If you do not have a Crock-Pot, run to the nearest retail store or thrift store and get one *now*. They are time-savers, and we cannot stress how much you will learn to love a slow cooker or Crock-Pot. Also, pay attention to the grocery list and the grocery tip system we included, plus our tips on *how to organize your cupboards, refrigerator and freezer in the section called "organizing the tightwad way."*

Now, let's get cookin' with the four main food groups: *canned, frozen, boxed and takeout!*

—Tightwad Twin Susan, the better cook

OUR TWO CENTS

Sometimes when we go to the beauty shop, we just go in for an estimate.

P.S. Ann's favorite recipe: Mix everything from the left side of the refrigerator with everything from the right side of the refrigerator. Cover with crumbled potato chips and bake.

I have won awards on office organization unlike some people I know. So, in this chapter, *I* have divided the recipes into the word, RECIPES for easy finding.

R . . . Really fast stews, soups and sandwiches
E . . . Easy Crock-Pot recipes
C . . . Canned . . . dump and lump
I . . . Innovative simple desserts
P . . . Potatoes, potatoes, potatoes
E . . . Easy tips and skillet, pan and oven dishes
S . . . Salads and snacks

Really Easy Stews, Soups and Sandwiches

Chili Crock-Pot

Dump leftover hamburger meat, 2 cans of cheap chili, 1 whole can of tomato juice and 2 cans of kidney beans in your Crock-Pot; cook on low all day.

Vegetable Soup

Dump leftover steak or hamburger meat into Crock-Pot, with 1 can of tomato juice, 2 cans of mixed or frozen vegetables, leftover potatoes or 2 cans of sliced canned potatoes.

A PENNY FOR YOUR THOUGHTS

It is better to eat soup with someone you love than steak with someone you hate.

—Proverbs, 15:17

Easy Potato Soup

Dump canned whole or sliced potatoes in the Crock-Pot; add any cream soup. Cook on low all day. Salt to taste.

Homemade Chicken Noodle

Dump cans of inexpensive chicken noodle soup with cans of chicken in a large pot on the stove. Cook on the stove on low until hot, or this can be done in the Crock-Pot on low all day.

Macky Chili

Dump canned macaroni and cheese or canned noodles with any leftover chili or cans of chili. Throw some Italian

> ## OUR TWO CENTS
> Susan recommends that instead of using a bit of flour on the bottom of a cake pan, save a bit of the cake mix . . . less messy than flour. Ann says to go to the bakery and pick out a cake. They'll even decorate it for you.

breadsticks in a plastic bag in the microwave and cook about 30 seconds.

Easy Chowder

Add ½ cup of Green Giant canned or frozen corn to canned potato soup and sprinkle with bacon bits.

Zesty Soup

Liven up tomato or chicken noodle soup with canned or frozen carrots, corn, peas, green beans, broccoli or cauliflower florets.

Cheese Broccoli Soup

one 8-oz. jar of Cheese Whiz
one can of cream of celery soup
  (condensed)
one 1 lb. pack of frozen broccoli
one 16-oz. carton of half and half

Mix and heat on low for about 2 to 3 hours until broccoli is tender.

> ## OUR TWO CENTS
> If we are what we eat, then we are fast, cheap and easy.
> (AT LEAST ANN IS)

Easy Crock-Pot Meals

HAVE YOUR MEALS READY WHEN YOU GET HOME!

Hint: Save all leftovers and freeze them.
You can use them in the soup section!

Bread Trick

Do you have leftover corn bread, already cooked rolls or leftover baked bread of any kind (even Italian bread sticks)? Wrap your bread with a double layer of aluminum foil. Turn your Crock-Pot lid upside down and place your bread on top of the lid. It does not matter if the handle of the lid dips into the Crock-Pot a little. Your bread is warm and ready to eat when your Crock-Pot meal is done.

For hot bread with your Crock-Pot meals, simply turn the lid over and place bread in aluminum foil on top.

Rumpy Roast

Dump a roast in the Crock-Pot, then lump it with canned sliced or canned whole potatoes, canned carrots or bagged peeled carrots and 1 can of cream of mushroom soup. Season to taste. Cook on low for 7 to 8 hours or until it registers 350 degrees on a meat thermometer.

Bar Potatoes

Baked potatoes in a Crock-Pot!

Wrap unpeeled potatoes in aluminum foil and place in a Crock-Pot with ½ cup of water. Cook on low for 4 to 8 hours, depending on the number of potatoes used. (Or you can cook on high for 2 to 4 hours.) Have your fixings already in containers in the fridge.

OUR TWO CENTS

Susan says to brush a bit of egg white on your pie crust to make it shine. Ann says that the Mrs. Smith's frozen pie box says nothing about doing that.

Ribby Meal

In the Crock-Pot, dump the country-style or regular-style ribs and lump half to a whole bottle of your favorite BBQ sauce. You may need to add some water.

Corned Beef and Cabbage

A complete meal in the Crock-Pot! Dump a can of corned beef into the Crock-Pot. Lump cabbage on top. Add about a coffee mug of water. Cook on low all day.

Chicken Stroganoff

Dump chicken breasts in the Crock-Pot. Lump 1 large container of sour cream, 1 can of cream of mushroom soup, 1 packet of onion soup mix and cook on low about 6 hours. If you need to cook for 8 hours, add some water. DON'T EVEN COOK NOODLES WHEN YOU GET HOME! Buy noodles in a can or serve with any leftover rice, if desired.

Beverly's Creamy Broccoli Chicken

1 can cream of broccoli soup
boneless breasts of chicken
* (as many as you need)*

1 cup milk
extra bag of frozen broccoli,
* if desired*

Place chicken in the Crock-Pot. Cover with frozen veggies, cream of broccoli soup and milk. Salt and pepper to taste. Cook on low all day (8 to 10 hours) or high 4 to 6 hours. Serve over rice. Yummy!!

Green Bean Casserole

Combine in a greased Crock-Pot three 10-oz. packages of frozen cut green beans or 3 cans of green beans; two $10^{1}/_{2}$-oz. cans of cheddar cheese soup; $^{1}/_{2}$ cup water. Add onion salt, pepper and salt to taste. Cover and cook on low 8 to 10 hours or high for 3 to 4 hours.

Broccoli Rice & Chicken

2 lbs. chicken tenders or
* boneless breasts*
1$^{1}/_{4}$ cups uncooked converted
* rice*

1 package Knorr's Cream of
* Broccoli Soup Mix*
1 can chicken broth
pepper, to taste

Place rice and chicken in a lightly greased Crock-Pot. Mix in the soup mix and broth. Cover and cook on low for 6 to 8 hours.

Chicken & Corn Bread Stuffing Casserole

4 to 6 boneless chicken breasts
1 small box Stove-Top Corn Bread
   Stuffing
One 10-oz. package frozen chopped
   broccoli (or mixture of broccoli
   & other veggies), thawed

1 can cream of broccoli with
   cheese soup
1 can chicken broth

OUR TWO CENTS
Blessed are those
who hunger or thirst,
for they are sticking
to their diets.

Mix the ingredients
together, cover and cook
on low 6 to 7 hours.
Absolutely delicious
comfort food!

Canned Goods—Open, Dump, Cook!

Mixed-Up Casserole

Dump 1 can mixed vegetables, 1 can of cream of mushroom
soup (or any cream soups you have on hand) and 2 cans macaroni and cheese (or leftover noodles) in a casserole dish. Cook
for 30 minutes at 350 degrees. Add cheese on top if desired.

"Fishy" Casserole

Dump and lump together: 3 cans of tuna fish, canned
noodles (or leftover noodles or rice), 1 can of cream of
mushroom soup (or any cream soups). Cook in a casserole
dish for 30 minutes at 350 degrees. Add cheese if desired.

Hashy Meat Casserole

Combine 1 package of hash browns, any leftover meat you have and 1 can cream of mushroom soup (or any "cream of" soups). Bake for 30 minutes at 350 degrees.

Doggy Mac Bake

Dump canned macaroni and cheese in a casserole dish. Add hot dogs in small bits or whole. Kids will love it!

Ham & Greeny Beany Casserole

Dump canned green beans in a casserole dish. Lump in leftover ham and any cream of mush-room, celery, chicken, or potato soup. Bake for 30 minutes at 350 degrees. Add cheese (sliced, packets or shredded) later if desired.

OUR TWO CENTS

Susan says to put a bit of apple in your potato bag to keep the spuds from budding. Ann says that this is unnecessary—the Hungry Jack potato mix will stay good in the pantry for over a year.

Green Bean Casserole

1 can cream of mushroom soup
3 cans of French-cut green beans or leftover green beans
1 can French-fried onions or 1 cup cracker crumbs

Mix and cook in a casserole dish at 350 degrees for 30 minutes. Add dried onion rings or cracker crumbs on top.

Green Bean and Turkey Casserole

1 can turkey or chicken
1 (14¹/₂-oz.) can Green Giant Cut Green Beans, drained
1 (10³/₄-oz.) can condensed cream of mushroom soup
¹/₃ cup milk

6 servings Hungry Jack Mashed Potatoes (prepared as directed on package) or leftover potatoes
1 (2.8-oz.) can French-fried onions
3 slices cheese

Heat oven to 375 degrees. In medium saucepan, combine meat, green beans, soup and milk; mix well. Add cheese; stir until melted. Pour into ungreased 2-quart casserole. Top with mashed potatoes. Bake at 375 degrees for 10 minutes. Sprinkle with onions.

More Quick Fixin's

Bake frozen chicken patties; top with a jar of pizza sauce and shredded mozzarella cheese.

Wrap grilled chicken and cooked Spanish rice (from a can) in a flour tortilla.

Mix cubed or canned chunk chicken, macaroni and cheese, and cooked mixed vegetables for a quick casserole.

Combine your favorite frozen Green Giant vegetables with refrigerated alfredo sauce and serve over pizza.

Spaghetti or alfredo sauces can be easily heated and poured over cooked pasta.

Cooked broccoli or asparagus is also delicious topped with alfredo sauce.

Stir refrigerated pesto sauce into your favorite cooked vegetables.

TIGHTWAD TRUTH
Calories in food used for psychiatric or medicinal purposes do not count.

Beefy Vegetables

1 can of vegetable beef soup
One bag of frozen vegetables or *any leftover vegetables*

Cook in saucepan on low until vegetables are tender.

Innovative Simple Desserts

Jell-O in a Jiffy

ALWAYS have a large Jell-O made each week. Then you can have it available for snacks or for desserts. Add raisins for eyes, miniature marshmallows noses and a small peeled carrot for a mouth! You can make these in advance.

Angel Cake to the Rescue

Buy an angel food cake. Add lumps of ice cream in the middle when ready to serve, or add whole strawberries or blueberries in the middle, or even canned fruit. You can also

OUR TWO CENTS

Cookie pieces
contain no calories.
The process
of breaking causes
calorie loss.

swirl chocolate syrup over the cake. Or just dump some jam or jelly in the middle of the angel food cake!

Big Cookie

Buy frozen cookie dough. Make a cookie as big as your cookie sheet. Bake according to the directions. Decorate if desired. It's ready for easy snacking all week or weekend long! Now that is ONE BIG COOKIE!

Ice-Cream Pie

1 quart vanilla ice cream (softened until mushy)
9 whole graham crackers, coarsely broken
14 bite-size chocolate bars (plain, crunchy, or nut), coarsely
* broken (or 3 regular bars)*
chopped unblanched almonds or walnuts
1 prepared 9-inch chocolate or graham cracker crumb crust.

Spoon the ice cream into a large bowl and gently fold in the graham crackers, chocolate bars and almonds. Spoon the mixture into the crumb crust and smooth the top. Garnish, if desired, with additional crackers, chocolate bars and almonds. Freeze until firm—about 2 hours. Serves 8–10.

Sun Cake

Surround a round cake with ladyfingers and wafer cookies.

Funky Craft Dough You Can Eat

1 cup butter or margarine softened	2 ½ cups sifted powdered sugar
6 hard-cooked egg yolks, mashed	2 tsps. baking soda
2 tsps. cream of tarter	1 tbsp. vanilla extract
5 cups all-purpose flour	Red, yellow or green paste food coloring
1 cup shortening	

Cream butter and shortening; add sugar, beating until light and fluffy. Add the egg yolks, soda, cream of tarter and vanilla, beating well. Add flour a little at a time, mixing well.

Divide the dough into 4 equal parts. Color one part red, one yellow, one green, and leave the last dough part plain. Wrap each part up separately in plastic wrap and chill at least 1 hour.

Here's the part the children love! They can hand-shape the dough into anything they want, or roll out the dough and cut it with cookie cutters. Bake their creations at 350 degrees degrees for 8 to 10 minutes. Let the cookies cool on the baking sheet for a few minutes.

Dirt Cups with Worms

2 cups cold milk
1 pkg. chocolate pudding
One 8-oz. tub whipped topping,
    thawed

One 16-oz. pkg. chocolate
    sandwich cookies, crushed
8 to 10 plastic 7-oz. cups

Pour milk into large bowl, add the pudding mix, beat until well blended. Let sit 5 minutes or so. Stir in the whipped topping and $\frac{1}{2}$ of the crushed cookies. Place 1 tbsp. crushed cookies into the cups. Fill the cups $\frac{3}{4}$ full with the pudding mixture. Top with remaining cookies. Refrigerate 1 hour. Decorate with gummi worms and frogs.

Take our word for it, they look rather disgusting but the children love them!

Pokey Cake

Bake a cake as usual. Poke holes in the top with an ice pick or with skewers and pour cooked gelatin into the holes. Use any colors that you desire. Red and green would be fantastic for Christmas. Other colors/flavors would be good for birthday cakes.

Heavenly Angel Cakes

Try these four ideas:
• Cut a whole angel food cake in half crosswise, take off the top, and spread with whipped cream and sliced berries of your choice. Replace the top and crown with more cream and berries.
• Toast slices of cake and add ice cream and any topping of your choice (chocolate, strawberry, etc.)
• Serve each angel food cake slice in a liquid pool of fruit

puree or any sauce that you desire. Add fresh fruit around the side of each plate.

- Tear angel food cake in pieces and layer in your favorite bowl. Pour on pudding and/or sliced fruit and repeat the steps of layering. Top with whipped cream.

Basic Frosting for Spreading

¼ cup butter   *confectioner's sugar*
¼ cup milk

Melt butter and add milk. Beat in enough confectioners' sugar to make frosting thick enough to spread easily. This makes enough to frost one 9-inch layer cake.

A PENNY FOR YOUR THOUGHTS STORY: (FROM A READER)

Real Mothers

Real mothers don't eat quiche—
they don't have time to make it.
Real mothers know that their
kitchen utensils are probably in
the sandbox.
Real mothers don't want to know
what the vacuum just sucked up.
Real mothers don't question why
they sacrifice for their families.
They just know.

Basic Dark Chocolate Frosting

6 tbsps. softened butter or   2²/₃ cups confectioners' sugar
   margarine   ¹/₃ cup milk
³/₄ cup dark cocoa   1 tsp. vanilla

In a small mixing bowl, cream softened butter or margarine. Add cocoa and confectioners' sugar alternately with milk. Beat to a spreadable consistency. Add more milk as needed. Blend in vanilla. Makes about 2 cups of frosting.

Basic Decorator Frosting

¹/₂ cup shortening   2 tbsps. milk
1¹/₂ cups confectioners' sugar

Cream shortening with confectioners' sugar. Stir in milk. Beat well, adding more sugar as needed to make a stiff enough consistency for use in a pastry bag. Makes enough to frost one 9-inch layer cake.

Basic White Cake

2¹/₂ cups cake flour, sifted   1¹/₄ cups sugar
2¹/₂ tsps. baking powder   1 cup milk
¹/₂ tsp. salt   1 tsp. vanilla
¹/₂ cup butter   4 egg whites, stiffly beaten

Preheat oven to 375 degrees. Butter and flour pan. Combine cake flour with baking powder and salt. In a large bowl, cream butter and sugar. In a separate bowl, combine milk and vanilla. Add this and the flour mixture to the butter mixture alternately, beating after each addition. Gently fold in egg whites. Pour batter into pan. Bake for about 25 minutes, or until a toothpick inserted into the center comes out dry.

The Twins'
Apple-Pie-in-a-Hurry!

Dump apple pie filling into a prepared crust. The end.

Potatoes,
Potatoes, Potatoes

Mashed Taters

Dump frozen mashed potatoes in a greased casserole dish. Add frozen broccoli or asparagus on top. Bake for 30 minutes at 350 degrees. Add cheese if desired.

Easy Potato Salad

Dump canned drained sliced potatoes in a bowl. Refrigerate about 30 minutes. Add mayonnaise, salad dressing or mustard, if desired; add salt and pepper to taste.

Tater Tot Casserole

It only takes 2 minutes to go to the freezer and dump a bag of Tater Tots plus 2 cans cream of mushroom soup in a greased casserole dish with a bag of chicken nuggets or a box of fish sticks. Cook as directed for the Tater Tots.

Scalloped Potatoes

Dump canned sliced potatoes in the Crock-Pot. Lump 3 cans cream of potato, cream of mushroom or cream of celery soup. On top of this, lump the cheese packet that comes with the cheap mac and cheese or sprinkle on shredded cheese or sliced cheese before you serve.

Hot Potato Bar

Bake your potatoes. Use these for easy toppings:

TIGHTWAD TRUTH
Dinner is ready at Ann's house when the smoke alarm goes off.

- For Reuben Topping: Corned beef, Russian dressing, sauerkraut and Swiss cheese strips. Broil to melt cheese.
- For Chill-Out Chili Topping: Heated canned chili and top with shredded cheddar cheese and onion salt.
- For "Beachy" Topping: Drained, canned salmon or tuna, snipped fresh dill and heated frozen creamed spinach.
- For Oriental Topping: Heated canned chicken chow mein sprinkled with peanuts.
- For New York Deli Topping: Whipped cream cheese, sliced smoked salmon and a little bit of chopped red onion.
- For Healthy Topping: Shredded zucchini and carrots mixed with yogurt and chopped green onions.

Lisa's Famous Potato Soup

*8 cups coarsely chopped
  peeled potatoes
1 cup bacon bits
One 8-oz. pkg. cream cheese,
  softened*

*Three 14½-oz. cans chicken broth
One 10¾-oz. can condensed
  cream of chicken soup
Onion salt and pepper, to taste*

Mix all ingredients together, put in a covered pot or saucepan. Cover and cook the soup on low heat for 8 to 10 hours or on high for 4 to 5 hours or until potatoes are done.

Easy Tips and Skillet, Pan and Oven Dishes

Potato Trick

Peel your potatoes that you need for the week and cover the potatoes completely with salt
water. Now potatoes are ready to be thrown into the Crock-Pot in the morning before you go to work!

Inventory Trick

If you have a lot of noodles, go ahead and make them all up and refrigerate. Use them with your casseroles or reheat when you are too tired to cook them during the week. Same goes for rice packages!

Shepherd's Pie

1 can cut green beans	*2 tsps. cornstarch*
1 can green peas and pearl	*2 tbsps. cold water*
onion, not drained	*3 cups coarsely chopped leftover*
1 can carrots, sliced	*roast beef, pot roast or steak*
1 can chicken/beef broth	*1 pkg. frozen mashed potatoes*
Salt to taste	*Paprika to taste*

Mix and transfer all except potatoes to an ungreased 10-inch pie pan or quiche dish. "Frost" with the potatoes and sprinkle with the paprika. Slide the pie onto a baking sheet and bake, uncovered, for 15 minutes or until bubbling and lightly browned. Serves 4.

To make your own flavored tea, add lemonade, orange juice or cheap punch mixture.

Milk will last longer if you add a pinch of salt to it.

> **TIGHTWAD TRUTH**
> If anyone wants breakfast in bed at Ann's house, she tells them to sleep in the kitchen.

Buy imitation bacon bits to use on your food.

Always save and freeze your leftover stews, soups and chili to be added to other meals of the same.

Spam to the Rescue

Place four thick slices of Spam in a casserole dish standing up. Place pineapple slices in between each slice. Place leftover drained pineapple around the edges of casserole dish. Top with pineapple juice, brown sugar and dry mustard mix.

Bake at 350 degrees for 25 minutes. You might need to baste occasionally.

Fast Homemade Pizza

Create homemade pizza easily with Pillsbury Refrigerated All Ready Pizza Crust as a base, and any of these topping ideas:

- Refried beans, salsa, ripe olives and grated cheddar or Monterey Jack cheese.
- Pizza sauce, pepperoni slices, thin strips of green bell pepper and shredded mozzarella.

TIGHTWAD TRUTH

Writing down
what you buy will
shock you to
the sky!

(especially at the
grocery store)

- Pizza sauce; red, green, and yellow bell pepper strips; chopped onion and fresh mozzarella or provolone cheese.
- Pizza sauce, pineapple tidbits, Canadian bacon, chopped green bell pepper and shredded mozzarella.

For Cold Pizza: herb-seasoned soft cream cheese, coarsely chopped broccoli, green onions, tomatoes and fresh herbs.

Easy Nachos

To transform tortilla chips into party-hearty nachos, layer on some or all of the following:

- Old El Paso Refried beans
- Shredded Monterey Jack or your favorite cheese
- Chopped onions
- Minced jalapenos
- Chopped roasted bell peppers
- Chopped fresh tomato
- Sliced ripe olives
- Nonfat sour cream
- Old El Paso Salsa

Fresh Vegetable Pizza

One 8-oz. can Pillsbury
    Refrigerated Crescent
    Dinner Rolls
One 8-oz. carton dairy sour
    cream
Horseradish to taste

Salt and pepper to taste
1 small can mushrooms, chopped
1 tomato, chopped
1 pkg. small frozen broccoli
Onion salt to taste

Heat oven to 375 degrees. Separate dough into 4 long rectangles. Place rectangles crosswise in ungreased 15 x 10 x 1-inch baking pan; press over bottom and 1-inch up sides to form crust. Seal perforations. Bake at 375 degrees for 14 to 19 minutes or until golden brown. Cool completely. In a small bowl, combine remaining ingredients. Cut into appetizer-sized pieces. Store in refrigerator. Makes 60 appetizers.

What to Do with Leftover Rice

Mix leftover rice with shredded cheese. Stir in 1 jar pimentos and 1 package frozen green peas. Heat in microwave or cover and bake at 325 degrees in oven until hot.

Leftover Noodles

Toss leftover noodles with canned chunk chicken and frozen or canned veggies with bottled Thai peanut sauce.

Salads, Snacks & Drinks

Bean Salad

Dump equal cans of green beans and yellow beans, kidney beans into a large bowl. Mix with Italian dressing.

Dr. Pepper Salad

Dump together: 1 package cherry Jell-O, 2 small canned Dr. Pepper's heated in the microwave in a bowl, 1 small package soft cream cheese and some red canned drained cherries. Wonderful salad or dessert!

Five-Cup Salad

DON'T MEASURE. Just use a coffee mug for each ingredient. Dump in a large bowl:

1 cup marshmallows   *1 can mandarin orange slices*
1 cup coconut   *1 cup sour cream*
1 can pineapple tidbits or chunks

Mix together and use for salad, dessert, breakfast or snack. Make a large bowl each week. Watch it goooooo!

Shimmering Super Punch

Thaw two 12-oz. cans of frozen cranberry-raspberry juice, cocktail juice concentrate and chill two 1-liter bottles of orange-flavor carbonated water. Mix them just before serving. To make it shimmer, float spiced apple rings and stars cut from orange peel on the surface.

Quick Party Punch

2 quarts lime sherbet
three 1-liter bottles
lemon-lime soda or
ginger ale

OUR TWO CENTS
ANN AND I ARE NOT
GLUTTONS. WE ARE
"EXPLORERS OF
FOOD."

Just before serving, scoop softened sherbet into the punch bowl. Slowly pour the soda or ginger ale over the sherbet and it will fizz!

Cheap punch: Buy the colored punch in plastic jugs and add vanilla ice cream.

"Funny Fillings"

Add unusual ingredients to conventional sandwich filling:

- Add raisins, coconut, crushed pineapple or honey to peanut butter.
- Chopped nuts, celery, green pepper, pickle relish, olives, sunflower seeds and onions perk up tuna.
- Mix mashed banana, peanut butter and a little frozen orange juice concentrate together for an unusual bread spread.
- Cream cheese mixed with chopped celery, nuts and raisins creates a great sandwich. Put the filling on wheat bread.

Yummy Yogurt

Why buy the expensive yogurt with fruit on top? Use canned fruit and mix with plain yogurt.

Kool-Aid Kool Pops

Do invest in those frozen popsicle makers! Freeze Kool-Aid, orange juice, grape juice or apple juice with PLAIN WATER for a cool treat on a hot day!

Heavenly Hash Salad

1-pound can pitted sweet cherries
1 cup of seedless grapes or
  1 can of grapes
1 cup small marshmallows, and
  almonds, walnuts or pecans

¹/₄ cup mayonnaise
¹/₄ cup sour cream
1 tbsp. brown sugar

Mix all ingredients together. Refrigerate.

Pink Pigs

Use reconstituted powdered or regular milk and add cranberry juice to the milk for Pink Pigs.

Purple People Eater

Add grape juice to reconstituted powdered or regular milk and your children can become Purple People Eaters.

Pizzas in a Bowl

Lay canned biscuits out on a cookie sheet after you have pressed them into little bowl-like shapes. Add mixture of sauce, desired meat and top with cheese. Onions, peppers and seasoning is optional. Cook until biscuits are done.

Tooty Fruity Pizza

Buy a pizza crust. Spread it with seasoned tomato sauce or pizza sauce. Add any canned drained fruit that you desire. Cook until the pizza crust is done. Add shredded cheddar cheese the last 10 minutes or so of baking. Also great for breakfast.

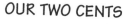

OUR TWO CENTS

If they don't
have chocolate
in heaven,
we ain't going.

Big Country Biscuit Wraps

One 12-oz. can Pillsbury Big
*   Country Refrigerated*
*   Buttermilk Biscuits*

1 can chunk ham
Shredded cheddar cheese,
*   as desired*

Heat oven to 400 degrees. Separate dough into 10 biscuits. Press each biscuit into 5-inch rounds.

Spoon ham and cheese onto center of each biscuit. Fold dough in half over filling; press edges with fork to seal. Place on ungreased cookie sheet. Bake at 400 degrees for 10 to 13 minutes or until golden brown. Makes 10 wraps.

Hungry Jack Jammin' Sandwich

*One 12-oz. can Pillsbury
    Hungry Jack Refrigerated
    Buttermilk Biscuits*
¼ cup strawberry jam
¼ cup grape jam
¼ cup apple jelly

Heat oven to 400 degrees. Place biscuits 2 inches apart on ungreased cookie sheet. Bake at 400 degrees for 8 to 11 minutes or until golden brown.

> **OUR TWO CENTS**
>
> Ann and I tried to exercise, but our thighs kept rubbing together and it slowed us down, but that doesn't matter . . . we're already in shape—we are round.

Split each biscuit into 4 layers. Alternating flavors, spread about 1 teaspoon jam or jelly between each layer. Makes 10 sandwiches.

An Ice Cream Tip

A marshmallow in the bottom of an ice cream cone helps absorb drips for young ice cream lickers!

Help from the Deli

Here are a few ideas to add to your next macaroni salad.

• Chopped fresh herbs
• Sliced ripe olives
• Chunks of tuna or cooked chicken
• Kidney beans, rinsed and drained

- Green Giant Niblets Whole Kernel Corn
- Capers or minced pickles
- Cheese cubes

NOTE: THE TIGHTWAD TWINS HAVE HAD TO TRY OUT EVERY ONE OF THESE RECIPES. IT WAS SUCH A JOB, ESPE-CIALLY THE DESSERT SECTION.

TIGHTWAD TRUTH

HUSBAND ASKS: "Can I help with dinner?"

WIFE HEARS: "Why isn't it already on the table?"

Before we leave this chapter, we'd like to share our favorite recipe for fruitcake. Read the whole recipe for a good laugh:

1 cup water	*1 tsp. salt*
1 cup butter	*1 cup brown sugar*
1 cup sugar	*2 cups flour*
4 large eggs	*1 tbsp. lemon juice*
2 cups dried fruit	*1 cup chopped nuts*
1 tsp. baking soda	*1 gallon cooking wine*

Sample the cooking wine to check for quality.

Take a large bowl.

Check the cooking wine again to make sure it is still okay.

Pour 1 level cup and drink.

Repeat if you are not sure of its quality.

Turn on the electric mixer and beat 1 cup butter in a large bowl.

Add 1 teaspoon sugar and beat again.

Make sure the cooking wine is still okay.

Cry another tup.

Turn off the mixer.

Break two legs and add to the bowl and chuck in the cup of drie dfruit.

Mix on the turner.

If the fried druit gets stuck in the beaters, pry loose with a drewdriver.

Sample the booking wine again to check for tonsisticity.

Next, sift 2 cups of salt, or something. Who cares.

Now sift lemon juice and strain the nuts.

Add 1 table. Spoon. Of sugar or flour or something white.

Whatever you can find.

Grease the oven.

Turn the cake pan to 350 degrees.

Throw one bowl out the window.

Check the wooking cine again.

Go to bed.

Who cares about dumb ol' cruitfake anyway?

YOU KNOW YOU'RE A TIGHTWAD . . .

. . . if your coupon file requires a room of its own.

Chef Boyardee is our new best friend! If you have not tried the *canned* macaroni and cheese, then you are missing a real treat and time-saver. Not only is it wonderful tasting and fast, but you can make about a million meals from this can as your base! For example, add cooked hamburger to it and you have hamburger and cheese casserole . . . add vegetables to it and it becomes a veggie casserole . . . add leftover ham to it and it is a ham and cheese casserole! Put in wieners and the kids will love it. . . . You can even just add bacon bits or other flavoring for another dish. The list can go on and on. Yes, we love Chef Boyardee for making this one. And the best part is that even Ann can do this recipe.

READER/CUSTOMER CARE SURVEY

We care about your opinions. Please take a moment to fill out this Reader Survey card and mail it back to us.
As a special **"thank you"** we'll send you exciting news about interesting books and a valuable **Gift Certificate.**

Please PRINT using ALL CAPS

First Name

MI.

Last Name

Address

City

ST

Zip

Phone # ( ) —

Fax # ( ) —

Email

(1) Gender:
___ Female   ___ Male

(2) Age:
___ 12 or under
___ 13-19
___ 20-39
___ 40-59
___ 60+

(3) Marital Status
___ Married
___ Single
___ Divorced/Widowed

(4) Did you receive this book as a gift?
___ Yes   ___ No

(5) How many Health Communications books have you bought or read?
___ 1   ___ 2-4   ___ 5+

(6) How did you find out about this book?
Please fill in ONE.
1) ___ Recommendation
2) ___ Store Display
3) ___ Bestseller List
4) ___ Online
5) ___ Advertisement
6) ___ Catalog/Mailing
7) ___ Interview/Review (TV, Radio, Print)

(7) Where do you usually buy books?
Please fill in your top TWO choices.
1) ___ Bookstore
2) ___ Religious Bookstore
3) ___ Online
4) ___ Book Club/Mail Order
5) ___ Price Club (Costco, Sam's Club, etc.)
6) ___ Retail Store (Target, Wal-Mart, etc.)

(9) What subjects do you enjoy reading about most? Rank only **FIVE.** Use 1 for your favorite, 2 for second favorite, etc.

	1	2	3	4	5
1) Parenting/Family	○	○	○	○	○
2) Relationships	○	○	○	○	○
3) Recovery/Addictions	○	○	○	○	○
4) Health/Nutrition	○	○	○	○	○
5) Christianity	○	○	○	○	○
6) Spirituality/Inspiration	○	○	○	○	○
7) Business Self-Help	○	○	○	○	○
8) Teen Issues	○	○	○	○	○
9) Sports	○	○	○	○	○

(14) What attracts you most to a book?
(Please rank 1-4 in order of preference.)

	1	2	3	4
1) Title	○	○	○	○
2) Cover Design	○	○	○	○
3) Author	○	○	○	○
4) Content	○	○	○	○

TAPE IN MIDDLE; DO NOT STAPLE

IıIIıııIIıIıIıIIııIıIıIIIIıIıIıIıIıııIIıIıIıI

FOLD HERE

Comments:

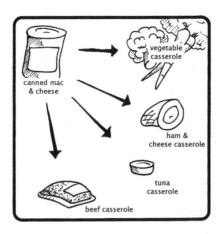

vegetable casserole

canned mac & cheese

ham & cheese casserole

tuna casserole

beef casserole

The Five Keys of Saving Money at the Grocery Store

M . . . Menu planning

O . . . Organization

N . . . Nevers, 4 of them

E . . . Eternal grocery list

Y . . . Yearly special events and holidays

Looks simple and it is. Let's look at each part more carefully. Keep in mind that this grocery plan can be for weekly shopping or shopping done less frequently. It even works with bulk buying which, of

OUR TWO CENTS

We finally got our heads together, but now our bodies are falling apart.

course, is the most economical way. The only problem with that method is that most tightwad families cannot afford bulk buying at times and live week to week and paycheck to paycheck.

MENU PLANNING: Now, we do not mean that you have to get fancy with this because we know your time is limited, but you can really get as detailed as you care to be. In fact, the more detailed and careful you are in this step, the more money you will save. Your list begins the big spending, so plan wisely. When we say menu planning, we are simply saying to jot down on your planning sheet the words breakfast, lunches, dinners, snacks and extras (special occasion food and items that week) divided into the days of the week . . . seven of them, not just five. Your family will need something there to eat for those weekend meals even if you do not have to cook. However, plan only for those days that most of your family will be home. For example, if you are going to Grandma's house for the day or weekend, you will not need to plan a lot for those days. Now, before you write one item down on that list, go to your kitchen and see what you have on hand and begin planning your little menus.

ORGANIZATION: This one is the key to saving BIG money! We spoke of this in the beginning of the chapter. We know that organization is a dirty word to some people, but it is a *must* if you want to save at the grocery store. On the form we have provided for your grocery shopping, we have also included the words: CALL, DO, BUY at the bottom. We did this because it can also become your weekly errand list all on the same sheet of paper! Got dry cleaning to pick up? Write it on the day to be done. Birthday party that week? Jot it down. Potluck at work? You are going to need extra food for that so include it all on one sheet. We do a new planning sheet every week. Whenever you reduce your life to ONE calendar and ONE buying/planning sheet, it is the road to a simpler life. We cannot function without our weekly planning sheet! We even write down due dates for upcoming bills that week, but to each his own.

NEVERS:

1. Never send your husband to the store unless you are one of the fortunate few who has a husband that will not buy impulsively and bring home name brand items that cost twice as much. Need we say more? Sorry, guys.

2. Never shop for your weekly groceries without your eternal grocery list! Enough said. . . . Just don't do it!

3. Never go back to the store if you can help it until your next weekly grocery-shopping trip comes around. If you do, then you did not plan well on your list. At first, you may have to do this, but try to plan everything you will need for the week. Why? Because every time you step into the grocery store, you spend money and even when it is for just one or two items you forgot, more times than not you will end up with five or six items. This is called a money leak and don't forget one of our truths: Small leaks can cause big ships to go down—fast or gradually. Either way, it will wreak havoc with your budget!

4. Never go to the store hungry, for obvious reasons. If you do, then run and get a candy bar to eat while shopping and

save the wrapper to pay for it at the end of the shopping trip. That candy bar will save you money in the long run!

ETERNAL GROCERY LIST: As mentioned earlier, we have one for you to copy in another chapter; but if you do not like ours, make up your own. You can copy the store aisle directory at the grocery and add to that. You will usually find these mounted on the cart. Simply slip it out and copy it on the machine there in the store, being sure to slide it back in the cart rack when you are finished copying it. Later, you can add to it and create your own weekly planning sheet and make more copies. The manager will not mind since he wants you to be happy shopping at his store. Some of our readers have gone the extra mile and made out their own list using the floor plan of their favorite grocery store; this way they can follow their list as the items come along instead of going all over the store with a list that is not divided according to the store lay-out. This will require a trip to the store and organizing the aisles as they come, but after it is done and copied, it saves a bunch of steps on your weekly shopping trips . . . a stitch in time saves nine . . . nag, nag.

YEARLY SPECIAL EVENTS AND HOLIDAYS: Keep your eyes peeled for those after-holiday specials that you can save for next year whether it be holiday napkins, holiday foods that are not perishable, or even some holiday gifts such as music, books, videos, etc. Of course, be sure to put these items in a gift place where you can actually see them to avoid duplicate buying at holiday times! Keeping a list of names by this gift place of what you bought and for whom would be invaluable. Shop also for a special buy such as birthdays and special events coming up, which you should also include on your grocery/planning sheet. To save even more money, try to buy different types of containers when purchasing your regular grocery items. For example, if you give your neighbors or coworkers candy at Christmas or special hot

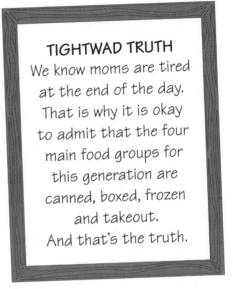

TIGHTWAD TRUTH
We know moms are tired at the end of the day. That is why it is okay to admit that the four main food groups for this generation are canned, boxed, frozen and takeout.
And that's the truth.

chocolate mixes, choose the olive or pickle jar that has a red top or a checked top so that you can recycle that jar into a gift container. Simply, add some ribbon, a calico swatch on top and a tag and it is done. You'll also find other interesting containers such as tins or boxes. Be sure to keep all of these containers, when they are empty and washed, near the same spot that you have organized your gifts so you can easily see what you have on hand.

Here are a few helpful hints that can save you money at the grocery store.

You don't have to eat meat *every* day. Try other foods such as beans, rice, pasta and vegetables.

Always serve *double* portions of fast fill-up foods such as potatoes, pasta, bread and rice.

Don't underestimate the value of the "dinner when you get home" appliance—the trusty Crock-Pot! (Please see twin Susan's hot bread Crock-Pot trick in the recipe section as well as "dump and lump" Crock-Pot recipes).

This one is important! If you are going to buy fast food, choose healthy items and include these items on your planning menu so you do not buy food at the grocery store for that particular meal. Look for fast food coupons and clip them to your planning sheet.

A Golden Nugget from Our Childhood

Our mama always made sure we had meat at every meal. Even if it was half a slice of bacon or a slice of Spam served with mountains of potatoes, it was still classified as a "meat and potatoes" meal. A few times we

> **TIGHTWAD TRUTH**
> Mothers are travel agents for guilt trips.

had fried bologna, and we thought it was neat because it curled up like a bowl. When we complained, which was rare, she told us about the starving children in the world. Sound familiar?

Here we are at our table, eating a "meat and potatoes" meal. Ann, of course, is the one with her mouth full.

Home and Car Maintenance

Growing up in a tightwad home as we did, we NEVER had a brand new car; however, we did learn a lot from our daddy about how to maintain a car no matter how used (or ugly) it might be!

Read on for some very informative home and automotive tips . . . by the way, why do appliances ALWAYS break down on the weekend?!!

Money-Saving Tips for Your Home

It's cheaper to paint older appliances than to buy new ones. There is special paint for them in your local stores (and some are heat-resistant).

Use old irons or bricks for bookends.

Pegboard and golf tees work for a bulletin board.

Make pincushions from scraps of bright fabric fitted tightly over steel wool balls. The steel wool will keep your pins sharp and in their place.

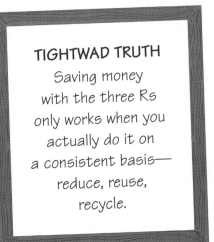

TIGHTWAD TRUTH
Saving money
with the three Rs
only works when you
actually do it on
a consistent basis—
reduce, reuse,
recycle.

Petroleum jelly solves the problem of a sticking sliding door when you rub some of it on the track and move the door back and forth to evenly distribute the jelly.

Line drawers with placemats that you don't use anymore.

To clean gunky grills and oven racks put them in a black plastic trash bag on a HOT sunny day. Pour a cup of ammonia into the bag, seal it and leave out to cook in the sun. A hose will wipe off most of the greasy crusties.

A plastic shower curtain or tablecloth in the truck of your car comes in handy if you have to kneel down in a dress suit to change a tire, check under the car or haul messy stuff.

Clear fingernail polish put on a loose cabinet knob will help it stay while you screw it back in.

Got a dead lawn mower? Remove the motor and top and replace it with a flat board to make a cart for hauling.

Roach killer: Mix $1/4$ cup shortening with $1/8$ cup sugar, $1/2$ pound of powdered boric acid and $1/2$ cup flour. Add a little water and make into balls. Place them in dark corners where children and pets cannot get to them (behind your refrigerator, stove, washer, dryer and in the back of your top cabinets).

Use baking soda mixed with water and a toothbrush for corroded battery cables.

Wash full loads rather than small loads. It saves on your water bill and also is less wear and tear on your washer and dryer.

Fix the drips in your house. A leaky hot-water faucet can waste up to 800 gallons of water a year.

OUR TWO CENTS

The Tightwad Twins' Daily Prayer

Lord, help us to relax
about insignificant details such
as the one coming at exactly
8:24 A.M. tomorrow.

Lord, help us not to
be such perfectionists
(did we spell that correctly?)

Lord, help us to slow
downandnotrushthroughwhatwedo.

Lord, help us to be open
to each other's ideas, WRONG
as they might be.

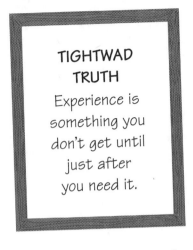

TIGHTWAD TRUTH

Experience is something you don't get until just after you need it.

Take a shower instead of a bath for water savings.

If you just need to wash your hair, use the sink and not a whole shower.

If you have a choice, use fluorescent lights. They provide three times the light of regular bulbs.

When buying lampshades, choose thinner lamp shades instead of the thicker ones for more light, thus less electricity.

Arrange your room so that one light will work for the entire room—even when you use lower-watt bulbs.

Do not block your vents with furniture.

Close your drapes and blinds to keep the sun's heat out in the summer and the heat in for the colder months.

Call your power company about a free energy audit. Many companies will insulate pipes and install low-flow shower heads at no charge.

For every degree above 65°F on your thermostat, you will be adding 3 percent to your heating bill.

In the summer, for every degree below 77°F, you will be adding 7 percent to your air-conditioning bill.

Dimmer switches can multiply bulb life up to twelve times while reducing electricity usage.

To fool a burglar, cut out the middle of an old book and put some of your treasure inside. Place the book among your other books.

Check your junk mail for envelopes to reuse, magazine pictures and coupons.

COMMON CENTS

THINGS YOU WILL NEVER HEAR A MAN SAY:

1. You know, that woman is just too well-endowed.
2. Sometimes I just want to be held.
3. Let's go to the mall and shop. I'll hold your purse.
4. Great! Your mother is coming again!
5. Sure, I will be happy to discuss the state of our relationship.
6. Honey, I'm going to the store. Do you need any feminine products?
7. Eat something! You look like a Victoria's Secret model!
8. Happy anniversary!
9. This movie has too much nudity! And, finally, our favorite sentence that you will never hear a man say:
10. I understand.

Clothes only need a 10- to 15-minute wash cycle.

The best water-saver for the bathroom is a low-flow toilet.

The biggest consumer of hot water in your home is the shower. Older shower heads deliver up to 8 gallons per minute. Shop for a shower head that puts out 3 gallons or less per minute.

Front-load washers use 33 percent less water than top-load washers.

A faucet aerator can cut water use in half and save up to one hundred gallons a year per faucet. Aerators for kitchen and bath faucets can be found in most hardware stores. They cost between $3 and $10, and simply screw into your faucet nozzle.

Check your heat/air filters at least once a month during hot weather. Vacuum or replace if needed.

Cars

A T-shirt over a bucket seat and headrest in a car makes an instant protective seat cover/cooler.

Deal only with reputable car businesses.

Believe the sign, not the salesperson, when it says the car is being sold "AS IS."

Get a second opinion on major repairs.

Protect your transmission from careless damage. Don't allow transmission fluid to get too low.

Old panty hose make a great rag for removing the bugs from your car windshield.

Cola cardboard bottle holders are great as car totes to fill with crayons, small tablets, mini-cars, etc.

Choose a manual shift. You'll save the $500 to $1,900 that an automatic transmission costs. Maintenance bills should be lower and gas mileage is better, too.

Don't get lazy about changing your fluids.

Drop collision coverage on older cars.

OUR TWO CENTS

THE TOP FIVE WAYS YOU KNOW YOU BOUGHT A CHEAP CAR

5. Your tinted windows are also known as Hefty garbage bags.

4. You can only use valet services that offer valet pushing.

3. Your car stereo system often requires a new needle.

2. The rearview mirror says "Objects in mirror are better than this piece of junk."

And, finally, the number one way you know you bought a cheap car . . .

1. When you pass hitchhikers, they put their thumbs DOWN!

Car wash mixture: ½ cup liquid detergent, ½ cup baking soda, 1 gallon water. It only takes a cup of this solution in a bucket of warm water to wash a car.

Buy two insurance policies (like house and car) from one agency.

Buy radial tires. They cut your gas consumption because there is less friction for radials than for ordinary tires.

Buy a clear hall runner and cut for car mats. Hall runners have teeth on the underside and will match all colors.

Ask for a good-driver rate. In some states—including California, Michigan and North Carolina—good drivers cannot be turned down by the company of their choice.

TIGHTWAD TRUTH

As we've aged, we have noticed that our bodies need more repairs than our childhood family car!

Organizing the Tightwad Way

O ur mother was clean. Her house was always neat and straight; however, you had better duck if you opened a closet! To this day, we are fanatics about organization. Based on our mother's example, we may even need therapy!

Use a slatted side of an old crib and turn it lengthwise to hold magazines or towels.

By simply stacking old narrow coffee tables, you can create some great storage for your garage.

The old compact, when the mirror is broken, can be used for a pillbox, safety pins, hair pins, small hooks or even a toothpick carrier.

Save the plastic bowl-like bottoms of liter bottles. They make excellent containers for sponges and soaps.

Old wire album stands are great for saving folders, cardboard, notepads and papers by the phone area.

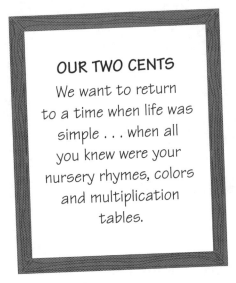

OUR TWO CENTS

We want to return to a time when life was simple . . . when all you knew were your nursery rhymes, colors and multiplication tables.

Flat box tops make excellent stack trays for papers.

Use the Styrofoam egg cartons for drawer organizers or emergency ice trays.

Save meat trays for painting or for messy projects. Wash the trays with soap and hot water first.

An empty cassette-tape container makes a great carrier for pins, pills, etc.

Save all used folders, notebooks, and index tabs to reuse for reports, school projects, gift tags, etc.

Organize your car trunk with personalized boxes for sports and school stuff.

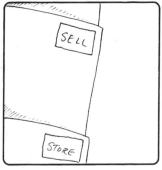

Organize your closets, garage or whatever with these labeled boxes.

To make flashlights last longer, place aluminum foil between the spring and the end cap.

Use toilet paper tubes for storing extension cords neatly.

When the adhesive on an envelope or a stamp fails and you don't have any glue, try some clear fingernail polish.

> **A PENNY FOR YOUR THOUGHTS**
>
> Angels don't run from life, they fly toward it . . . and so the flight of mothers.

Use the colored tops to aerosol cans for rubber bands, paper clips, earrings, Q-Tips, etc.

Getting rid of LPs? Use old album covers for file folders, or for sending photos or breakable items.

Old wooden pop bottle crates are just the right size for spice cans and jars.

An old tackle box makes a great sewing box, knickknack box, etc. Paint it! Add decals or cut out a design or flower from contact paper.

Save empty heart-shaped Valentine candy boxes for storage and for displays. You can paint them or decorate them.

Cover boxes with old flannel shirt material to make a container for your husband's personal items.

Outdoor twigs can be cut and nailed or glued onto containers to create a rustic desk set and organizers.

Spam cans or Pringles cans can be covered and/or painted to help organize a desk.

Old napkin holders make great card or bill organizers.

Save paper towel tubes for storing special drawings or pictures.

Hang a six pack ring on a hanger for scarves, belts, and ties.

Use an old belt to store hair bows and barretts. Just clip them on and hang the belt by the buckle on a hanger.

Use old socks as shoe covers.

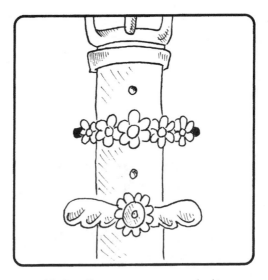

Hair-clip storage on a belt.

Thread a cord (perhaps from an old panty-hose elastic or sweat pants) through the casing end of a pillowcase— great laundry bag.

COMMON CENTS

DAILY SURVIVAL KIT

1. Toothpick: Pick out the good qualities in people.
2. Rubber bands: Be flexible.
3. Bandage: Heal hurt feelings—yours or someone else's.
4. Pencil: List your blessings every day.
5. Eraser: It's okay to make mistakes—everyone does.
6. Chewing gum: Stick with your project to the end.
7. Mint: You are a worthy person.
8. Candy kiss: Everyone needs a hug sometimes.
9. Tea bag: Relax and meditate on your blessings.
10. A mirror: Be the person you see there—be yourself.

Save old lunch boxes—they make great sewing kits, snack kits for the car, first aid stuff, cassette holders—the list is endless!

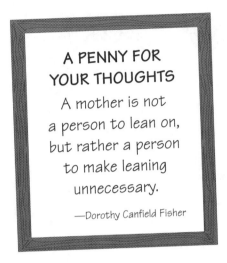

A PENNY FOR
YOUR THOUGHTS

A mother is not
a person to lean on,
but rather a person
to make leaning
unnecessary.

—Dorothy Canfield Fisher

Good packing material ideas are Styrofoam, Easter grass, crumpled newspaper, dry cleaning bags, and stale popcorn.

The old empty Band-Aid tin makes a neat emergency kit for your purse. Fill with a couple safety pins, some Band-Aids and a needle already threaded. Sister Char says to add a couple of headache powders for yourself!

The long boxes that hold little bags of chips are perfect for your photo envelopes—scoot them under a bed!

Don't throw away old tissue boxes or trash bag boxes with the hole in the top. Stuff your plastic grocery bags in these and use as a pop-up dispenser!

You can get as many wire hangers as you need in consignment shops. Most consignment shops freely give them away.

A pillowcase, opening at the top, can easily be folded over a hanger and secured with big safety pins, then used for a diaper holder or dirty clothes bag.

Organize your closet lists into categories: shoes, tops sweaters, accessories, etc.

When you get your yearly calendar, mark all important dates such as birthdays ahead of time. Also, pencil in any jobs you need to do that month such as spring cleaning and pencil in all of your appointments that you know of for the year such as yearly physicals, pet shots due, children's shots due, etc.

When moving, leave your clothes in the dresser drawers.

Use towels to cushion breakable items.

Use your answering machine as your personal phone call screener. Don't be chained to the phone.

Give your kids a snack while doing their homework. No play until homework is done. Use this time to get your outfit ready for work tomorrow and start dinner.

Use a timer for morning school-time showers when one or more kids are in the house. Setting time limits on showers avoids the rush to the bus and gives everyone a fair turn in the bathroom.

Assign a particular towel to each family member to keep all week.

Do certain jobs in certain months. When the season changes, wash windows, check fire alarms, etc., or in January, clean out closets, kitchen, cabinets, etc.

Consider hiring a teenager to help with dishes, laundry, etc. They work cheap, and you can keep your sanity.

Put appointments in one family calendar near the phone. Too many calendars create confusion.

Use your kitchen timer for deadlines to start or stop a given chore. It is much more fun to beat the clock. There is still a little bit of kid in all of us!

We love this trick. Use the circular plastic ring from the milk gallon jug or even the plastic rings from a six-pack canned drink to drape over a hanger hook, thereby creating a place to hang on another hanger. Saves closet space!

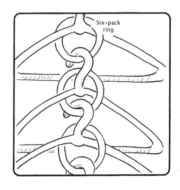

Double your space for your clothes using plastic six-pack rings to "stagger" your hangers.

Create ONE station for dirty laundry, preferably right by the washer. Label this station: WHITES, COLORS, DRY CLEAN or DELICATE. The laundry will always be sorted.

OUR TWO CENTS
"Freedom
of the press"
means no-iron
clothes.

Have TWO laundry baskets in the kids' rooms and in your room, one for whites and the other for colors. HINT: Buy a white laundry basket for whites and a colored laundry basket for colors.

Before bedtime, have each person take his or her dirty clothes to the laundry station.

Make Friday night your laundry night. What a feeling to wake up with no laundry to do on the weekend.

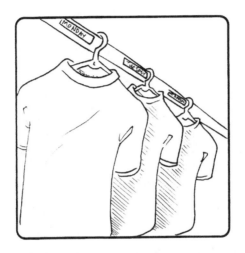

Label your child's closet rod with masking tapes labeled with the day and the outfit. Choose the outfits with your child all on one day to avoid morning squabbles.

Flower pots are cheap organizers that also come in a variety of colors and sizes.

Large trash bags hung over hooks on a garage wall make excellent recycling stations.

OUR TWO CENTS
There just cannot be a crisis this week. Our schedules are already full.

People throw old drawers away. Use them to slip under the bed to store items. They even have a handle!

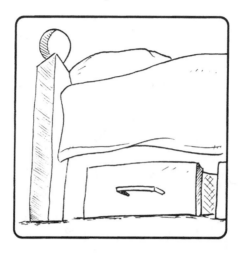

Nail old blue jean pockets on a board to organize anything. This is not only a great idea in the house and garage, but what a wonderful idea for a child's room.

A hanging shoe bag can organize almost anything, anywhere—from shoes to Beanie Babies to makeup.

Ask your grocery store for any display shelves they may be tossing out. Some are great for storing items, perhaps in your garage.

Old suitcases work perfectly for storing children's artwork or special papers.

A tall skinny wastebasket can makes an excellent, portable gift-wrapping station.

Cutlery trays can turn into desk drawer organizers or dividers for nuts and bolts.

Assign different-colored towel sets to each member of the family. When you see that towel on the bathroom floor, you'll know who the guilty one is.

COMMON CENTS

WARNING:
Dates on your calendar are closer than they appear!

IMPORTANT NAMES AND NUMBERS

	Name	Address	Phone Number
D Dentist/Orthodontist			
O Family physician			
C Ob/Gyn			
T Optometrist			
O Pediatrician			
R Veterinarian			
S Other			
Other			
U Cable TV			
T Electric			
I Gas			
L Oil			
I Garbage			
T Telephone			
I Water			
E Other			
S Other			

IMPORTANT NAMES AND NUMBERS *(continued)*

		Name	Address	Phone Number
S	AC/Heating			
E	Car care			
R	Electrician			
V	Pharmacist			
I	Plumber			
C	Yard service			
E	Other			
S	Other			
F	Accountant			
I	Attorney			
N	Banker			
A	Insurance agent			
N	Car			
C	Home			
I	Life			
A	Other			
L	Other			

Pets (Your "Furry and Finny" Family Members) and Outdoor Pests

Money-Saving Ideas for Pets

Save empty film canisters and fill with a small object for a great cat toy.

A two-liter bottle makes a great little fish tank. Decorate with fish stickers.

A good emergency pet carrier for your car is two laundry baskets—one tied atop the other one.

A plastic milk jug with the top cut off makes a wonderful scooper for pet food or for scooping out fertilizer from those big bags.

A dog sweater can be made from a regular sweater by cutting off the sleeves. Cut holes for arms, legs, underside.

Outdoor Living

A good idea for a bird feeder or a birdbath is an angel food cake pan or bundt pan filled with water and a plastic cup placed in the hole filled with birdseed. Nail or attach at a high level to house or shed pole.

Get rid of weeds or unwanted grass between patio bricks or sidewalks by spreading salt on them.

Stack bricks three high to form a circle. Add an old oven rack or grate to the top and you have a barbeque pit!

Save your rectangular cartons for birdhouses—paint and make a stick or button roof.

Don't throw away leftover popcorn, freeze it. Then sprinkle it outside during snowy days. The birds love it!

Aspirin tablets, pennies or ice cubes in water will lengthen the life of freshly cut flowers.

Take old rake or broom handles that you may find in other people's trash and use them as stakes for your garden.

Old panty hose make wonderful ties for holding up tomato plants. Wet weather makes them even stronger.

Deer don't like panty hose or pet hair! The next time you get your dog groomed, ask the groomer to save your dog's hair for you. Place it in a pair of panty hose and tie it up in your garden. Deer will not come near it.

Save those pizza boxes. They can be forms for concrete. Line the pizza box with clean plastic wrap. Pour in concrete mix and let it dry. Then peel away the box.

A barrel with a hole in the middle of the top and filled with rocks or sand makes a great little outdoor table. Put a patio umbrella in the hole.

Wooden pallets can make a good fence in a pinch.

Make a tiny birdhouse from cottage cheese or margarine containers.

For a small watering system, punch holes in a cut-off milk jug and place in a garden.

Use milk jugs for little greenhouses or protective covers for smaller plants against the cold.

You can spend a fortune and a lifetime fighting pests. Here are a few tips we've learned:

- Use hair spray on fleas, bees and insects in the house. It stiffens their wings for easier swatting.
- Take a lump of sugar and wet it with several drops of spirits of camphor bought at a pharmacy when outdoors for mosquito problems.
- Instead of expensive ant products for outdoor storage areas, use cucumber peel on a shelf or in a drawer to ward off ants.
- To keep cats out of your garden, sprinkle orange peels.
- Instead of sprays on cockroaches and ants, wash or spray cabinets with equal parts of vinegar and water.
- Put peppermint around all entrances to your house. Bay leaves can be used around the pantry to keep pests away.
- Soapsuds can be used as an insecticide in a spray bottle.
- Putting a garlic clove in plant pots repels plant pests.

YOU KNOW YOU'RE A TIGHTWAD . . .

. . . if you thought L.L. Bean
was a seed company.

PART TWO

FUN AND GAMES:
Sprucing Up and Getting Creative with Tightwad Style

Beauty, Clothing, Health and Travel

Our mother had beautiful skin and didn't spend a fortune on fancy or expensive beauty products. She simply washed her face every morning and night with baby lotion— generic lotion at that! She not only taught us that beauty is skin deep, but that it does not have to be expensive!

Buy inexpensive plastic pencil pouches for travel and organization of cosmetics—much cheaper than makeup bags!

Re-sole worn shoes for a few dollars. The shoe-repair shop can also repair luggage and handbags.

Don't buy expensive teeth-whitening products. Use $1/4$ teaspoon each baking soda and salt mixed in your hand or a container, add enough hydrogen peroxide to make a paste, then brush.

Get your immunizations free! Most local health departments do this for free, and there are no income limits. They are the same shots you pay $30 for at the doctor's office.

OUR TWO CENTS

Sometimes when we go to the beauty shop, we just go in for an estimate.

Cut a slit like an "X" in an empty prescription bottle bottom for a toothbrush holder for traveling.

Vests are professional looking and much cheaper than blazers. Reversible vests are a double savings.

All cream and all black always look expensive and tasteful.

Wear tights instead of panty hose in the winter—they are warmer and last a lot longer. Some are cheaper than panty hose.

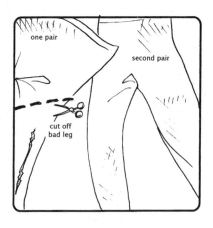

On the Maury Povich Show and the Crook and Chase Show, we did a trick with panty hose; cut one bad leg of two pair of panty hose and insert the good leg of a pair inside the hole of the other good-legged pair of panty hose and you have a good pair of panty hose in an emergency. This is why it is good to always buy the same shade of panty hose.

You probably know that dry-cleaning costs can slowly bleed you dry. Five dollars per week = $260 per year. Try to avoid buying garments that have to be dry-cleaned.

Don't throw away out-dated silk ties. Cut the ends from the large end for a suit-pocket handkerchief.

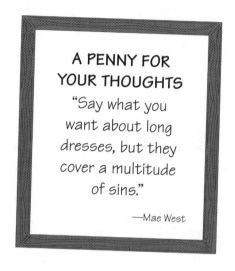

A PENNY FOR
YOUR THOUGHTS

"Say what you want about long dresses, but they cover a multitude of sins."

—Mae West

Cut the top from control-top panty hose for a comfortable everyday girdle.

Stretch your expensive perfume with a
"one-drop" perfume body spray.

OUR TWO CENTS

We heard a well-known homemaker on television say that her surefire cure for a headache is to take a lime, cut it in half and rub it on your forehead. We say take the lime, mix it with tequila, chill and drink.

Extend the life of your black shoes by using a black permanent marker on scuff-marks.

Don't be shy about adding little flowers, or even sequins, to dress-up shoes. They can be used for all occasions.

Add a short veil to headbands or other headpieces as a beautiful accent piece for a flower girl or bridesmaid.

Cut out the foot of an old sock and use it as a bandage to hold an ice pack for an injury or to hold a bandage in place.

Use a toothpick as an emergency "screw" for your glasses.

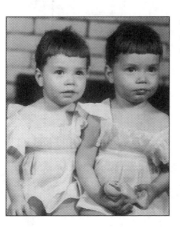

Mom cut our bangs to save money . . . Can you tell?

GET THE MOST OUT OF YOUR MOVEMENTS

FUN ACTIVITY	Minutes to Burn 100 Calories
Aerobics (high/low impact)	10
Baseball	25
Basketball	13
Bicycling (6 mph)	26
Bicycling (12 mph)	11
Bowling (non-stop)	38
Calisthenics	26
Canoeing (leisure)	40
Dancing (slow)	34
Dancing (fast)	12
Gymnastics	26
Horseback riding	15
Ice skating	20
Jogging (5 mph)	13
Jumping rope (moderate)	16
Rollerblading	22
Rowing (moderate)	22
Running (7.5 mph)	8
Running (10 mph)	6
Sailing	32
Skiing (cross country)	10
Skiing (downhill)	13
Skiing (water)	17
Soccer	17
Squash	13
Stationary cycling (10 mph)	16
Swimming (back stroke)	22

FUN ACTIVITY	Minutes to Burn 100 Calories
Swimming (crawl)	28
Tennis (singles)	16
Tennis (doubles)	26
Volleyball	34
Walking (3 mph)	27
Walking (4 mph)	18
Walking upstairs (1 step per sec)	14
Watching television	77
Weight training (light)	20

"YUKKY" ACTIVITY	Minutes to Burn 100 Calories
Cleaning	27
Cooking	36
Dusting	41
Food shopping	30
Ironing	53
Making beds	41
Mowing lawn (manual)	25
Mowing lawn (power)	29
Shoveling snow	15
Typing	59
Vacuuming	17
Washing floors	27
Washing windows	26
Weeding garden	19

Travel List

Clothing

____ Belts	____ Jeans	____ Slips
____ Blouses	____ Robe/pajamas	____ Socks
____ Bras	____ Scarves	____ Stockings
____ Coat	____ Shirts	____ Suits
____ Dresses	____ Shoes	____ Sweaters
____ Gloves	____ Skirts	____ Swimsuit
____ Gowns	____ Slacks	____ Ties
____ Hats	____ Slippers	____ Underwear
____ Jackets/raincoat		

Toiletries

____ Aftershave	____ Makeup	____ Shaving kit
____ Blow dryer	____ Eye makeup	____ Soap
____ Brush and comb	____ Blusher and	____ Sunblock
____ Creams/lotions	brush	____ Talc
____ Curling iron	____ Foundation	____ Toothbrush/
____ Dental floss	____ Powder	toothpaste
____ Deodorant	____ Manicure items	
____ Feminine needs	____ Mouthwash	
____ Hair ornaments	____ Perfume	
____ Hair spray	____ Razor	
____ Lipstick	____ Shampoo, rinse	

Medical

____ Adhesive bandages	____ Prescriptions and necessary
____ First-aid ointment	nonprescription medications
____ Glasses: extra pair	____ Thermometer
____ Insect repellent	____ Vitamins

Miscellaneous

____ Address book	____ Flashlight	____ Sewing kit
____ Alarm clock	____ Jewelry	____ Stamps
____ Camera and film	____ Pen	____ Sunglasses
____ Cash/travelers' checks	____ Reading material	____ Travel tickets
____ Checkbook	____ Safety pins	____ Umbrella
____ Credit cards	____ Scissors	(purse-size)

YOU KNOW YOU'RE A TIGHTWAD . . .

. . . if you have your hair done by people who wait
for instructions from the teacher.

Homemade Crafts
and Gifts

We are not great crafters. You can always tell when we have made something; however, we enjoy doing it and offer these tips for those of you who know what you're doing!

A piece of lace draped over a jar and the lid over the lace makes not only a wonderful accent in your room, but also great for presenting homemade goodies.

Some artificial flowers are ugly. Save the good parts from these, and when you have enough, glue them around a framed picture or mirror. If they are still ugly, spray-paint them all white, gold or silver.

Real leaves make great natural stamps to "spruce" up (pardon the pun!) packages or gifts during the fall or spring seasons. Simply dip the leaves in paint and press onto paper, fabric or canvas.

How about a gift wreath for a friend who is a cook? Save that old wreath that you were thinking of throwing away and add some wooden spoons, can labels, forks and anything else you can get your hands on in the kitchen besides the kitchen sink!

If you have some old lingerie that you do not wear any longer, cut off the lace and decorative embroidery and use it to make small pillows, sachets or baby pillows.

Panty hose make wonderful stuffing for pillows and stuffed animals.

To make your own paper pulp to mold for crafts, mix cheap paper plates with water in a blender. Add water or more plates until you get the consistency you like.

Wine bottles, especially the green ones, look great as a stand for red candles.

Glue magazine pages onto cardboard and cut into puzzle pieces for hours of fun. Old photos are great for this, too.

Something as simple as an Alka-Seltzer box can make a great little house or manger for your Christmas scene.

Brown lunch bags can make elegant gift bags. Stamp them with gold images and top them off with a gold bow.

If you run out of small gift boxes and have larger boxes around, you can easily retrofit them. Take apart a small foldable gift box and use it as a pattern to make your own.

Before you throw away any garment, snip off all the buttons, elastic, zipper or decorations.

Save the seed packets used from your garden for decoupage projects.

Make a festive candleholder for a party or centerpiece using leaves. Simply tie the leaves to the outside of the candleholder with a ribbon.

After dinner is over, save those fancy paper lace placemats for craft projects.

Cut the corners off of used envelopes and use for your photo corners in your albums.

If you can braid hair, you can braid strips of fabric together to make rugs. Tie three long fabric strips to anything stationary, like a bedpost. Braid them. When you get to the end, begin another three-piece section. Then tie the sections together, wrapping them in a round or oval shape. End by wrapping with string or thread.

Use cheap aluminum foil for a silver-packaged gift.

Save old card fronts and the verses and messages inside the cards for future gift tags.

A great gift for any occasion: Fill a basket with bath soaps from the "dollar" store, bath oil, reading material, toys, games, sewing items, baby gifts, travel items, etc.

When buying gift wrap, get all-occasion print or colors. For example, red and white dots can be used for Christmas, Valentine's Day and birthdays.

Buy a bundle of firewood and tie with a large red ribbon for the hostess who has a fireplace.

Use Styrofoam trays for gifts of food, such as chocolate, cookies or other sweet treats, then wrap in colored plastic and add a bow and a homemade tag.

Wallpaper samples make excellent bookmarks.

Photo blowups that can be done cheaply at discount stores make great gifts.

Good on the computer? See a poem you like? Type it on the computer, add your graphics, etc., and print out on paper that matches the décor in your recipient's home. Frame and give as a special gift.

A small, inexpensive address book is the perfect gift for a student going away to college.

Wrap a household shower gift with a kitchen towel. A scouring pad can be the bow.

Keep a box of gift-wrapping items: anything you possibly can use from those gifts you receive. Recycle tags, ribbons, flowers, paper.

Cocoa cans, baking powder cans, or any other can with a removable pry-off or screw-top cover can be converted very easily into useful banks.

Mouthwash tops or hairspray caps make great votive candleholders (you may want to put a little foil inside).

If you don't make your own gifts, at least make life easier by ordering from a catalog and having the company mail it to the person you are giving it to.

Printing shops throw away odd sizes of paper. Use for cards, arts and crafts projects, children's school projects and bookmarks.

YOU KNOW YOU'RE A TIGHTWAD . . .

. . . if burlap was the fabric of your choice
for Aunt Lucy's casket.

Furniture and Decorating

So many people throw out so much stuff! There is no excuse for not taking advantage of this fact and recycling some items that will work for your home. Our daddy demonstrated many of these in our childhood home.

- A bookshelf makes a wonderful headboard for a bed and frame. Just nail it on the wall at the right height for the bed.

- Never throw away the mattress to a sleeper sofa that has seen better days. The mattress is a good emergency for when guests come, and it can be stored under a regular bed.

- Almost anything can be turned into a desk. Concrete blocks and a door, a board and two smaller tables or two filing cabinets, or even stacked milk crates!

- To make an inexpensive table, top a clean garbage container or a large basket with a round or square piece of wood. Drape or paint. Great for storage, too.

TIGHTWAD TRUTH
If you can't glue it,
we don't do it.
If you have to sew it,
we'd rather throw it.

An attic room can be a wonderful bedroom for a teen or a guest or a child of any age. If the attic ceilings are too slanted to position a regular bed without someone knocking himself or herself out, use the mattress on the floor or cut the legs off of the regular bed. This works wonderfully!

Shelf Board

Mattress Board

Crate "bed" (cable-tie crates together;
you can also use concrete blocks).

Create a boxed bed by painting concrete blocks or crates (tied with cables) black (or any color) and top with a board. Place a mattress on top of the board for a modern bed look.

Mrs. Butterworth's syrup jars make great colonial-style vases.

For a cheap drafting table, cut down one end of a pair of

sawhorses equally (for the drafting table incline) and nail the desktop board you have chosen to the sawhorses.

For a bookshelf, use boards inserted into the steps of a ladder (or you can use two ladders) and paint or stain as you wish.

Another bookshelf idea is concrete blocks or bricks with boards placed on top of blocks. Use the block holes for knickknacks or small books.

Use everything from flower pots to large plastic cups to stack boards for extra shelves.

Yet another nifty idea for shelves comes from using boards stacked on top of flower pots or even large plastic cups.

To revamp an old trunk, table or box, cut out favorite magazine pictures. Glue on and cover with a brushed-on layer of equal parts white glue and water.

Add thumbtacks in a design along the side of an upholstered chair to create more interest.

Make a coffee table from an old window, door or board. Add bricks or flowerpots for legs.

Never underestimate the power of a little rubber band when creating those poof-ball, balloon curtains. Or if you have long drapes, slip the rubber band to the center of the drape and poof the upper part to cover the rubber band until you have the length that you desire.

Stuff the legs of old sweatpants and blue jeans for floor pillows. Secure the sections together with a ribbon.

Use pretty dish towels to cover that window in a kitchen back door or laundry room. Make slits for the rod to twine in and out.

Use napkins or scarves or bandannas, folded in half, points downward (like a row of banners), for a quick and pretty valance.

Tie two bandannas or pretty scarves together at the four corners to cover a tired pillow.

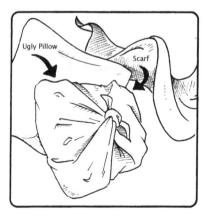

"Tie-scarf" pillow covers.

Ask your video store for their movie posters when they are done. Teenagers and kids love these for decorations. Also, the grocery store throws away a lot of items such as flowers, etc.

No curtain rod? Hang your country curtain over a taut piece of twine or attach it to the twine with little clothespins.

Gather fabric in a top knot with a rubber band. Cover rubber band with a ribbon. Hang on wall and drape the fabric around the head of a bed for a headboard.

Professionally trained color analysts have discovered that red generates energy, yellow builds creativity, green brings a feel of nature into a home, blue calms us, and purple is regal and classy.

Red is great for an accent color, especially in the kitchen, because it stimulates the appetite and mood.

Bright yellow is a color that can be stimulating in a room where you are working to keep up your visual energy and creativity.

Black for your home is much like a simple black dress. It can be elegant—or depressing. Use it with bright colors or white to keep the mood upbeat.

Green helps with the concentration level and is great for a home office.

Blue is great for a bedroom since it creates calmness.

> **TIGHTWAD TRUTH**
>
> Don't let your yearnings exceed your earnings!

Velvets and silks formalize a room—even a few pieces will have a dramatic effect.

Bright colors, added as accents to an all-white room really look great—almost like power bursts of color.

A plain tan doormat becomes festive by spray-painting a Christmas tree stencil around the edges. (You can cut simple triangle stencils out of any piece of thick cardboard.)

Trim the edge of a plain desk with pretty upholstery tacks.

Create your own decorative light-switch plates. Splatter-paint them, use decorative stickers, or glue on leftover wallpaper border or contact paper.

COMMON CENTS

Did you know that it takes 1 million years for a glass container to decompose in the garbage dump?
Did you know that Americans use enough Styrofoam cups per year to circle the earth 436 times? Unbelievable!
Recycling one ton of newspapers saves seventeen trees!

Get a hole-puncher and a Phillips-head screwdriver and punch a design into a dark-colored lampshade. Looks great when turned on at night. How about punching in your child's name or a holiday decoration in your favorite holiday lamp?

Be creative with tie-backs for your curtains. Use old belts, scarves, raffia, vines, old stringed beads, bandannas, lace, necklaces, etc.

For drawer handles, be creative! How about baby blocks, small balls or old doorknobs?

This is a super tightwad trick for outdoor shutters. If you cannot afford to buy real shutters, buy snap-together flowerbed fences. Mount them with small, slender nails.

Save even small swatches of lace and glue to a lampshade. You can also add old buttons or charms.

Silver and gold are cheap—in spray paint, that is. Use these colors to add a classy touch to anything.

Save all your old calendar pictures for future framing—dollar-store frames are cheap!

Cut leftover bathroom wallpaper into one-inch strips and paste on the blinds in the bathroom. Now the blinds will coordinate with the walls, and you won't need curtains.

Don't forget to save that old compact mirror (taken out of the compact) and use it as a reflective base for a votive candle.

Forget the needle and thread—use diaper pins to wrap a

foam cushion with material. Change it when you're bored with it.

Cut out the unworn middle of a worn braided rug and use it as a smaller area rug.

Choose one color to spray-paint various frames you've collected—now you have a more unified grouping.

No drapery or shower curtain hooks? Use twine or cord (matching your fabric), and loop it through the first hole, then over the rod, through the second hole, etc., alternating and in-and-out pattern.

Pages from old books and even new magazines can give you some beautiful, free prints suitable for framing.

If you can't afford fine-painted tiles, choose just a few tiles and mix with more inexpensive tiles to create a unique pattern or buy decals and put them on plain tiles.

Go outside in the woods and gather sticks or bendable pieces of twigs and tie with raffia. Looks great on the hearth.

Old shades can be rescued! Cut out a shape and glue it under the shade so that it will "come alive" when the light is turned on in the evening.

You can cut your own stencils from pieces of plastic that usually get thrown away—deli food containers, store packaging or old placemats. Stars, moons and leaves are all easy shapes to cut out with an Exacto-knife.

Spray-paint that old broom handle and use it as a curtain rod or quilt hanger.

The plastic runners that have "teeth" can be used on porch steps to prevent slipping in rain or snow. Nail (or glue) the cut-to-size pieces to the steps *with teeth side up.*

Use your leftover peel-and-stick tiles for cabinet bottoms and dollhouses.

Never buy shelf paper again. Use free wallpaper samples.

Wallpaper stores have discounted wallpaper sample books free. Besides shelf paper, you can make beautiful pictures if you cut out and frame parts of the paper. Also, wallpaper is great for collage and scrapbooking projects.

Old maps make great game boards. Old maps with a layer of clear contact paper also make great room décor. With a piece of glass over a map on a table, you have an interesting conversation piece.

A heavy plastic or steel bucket turned upside down with four or so top holes makes a great umbrella stand.

Cut eight placemat-size rectangles of leftover kitchen or dining room wallpaper and glue them together so they are reversible. Cover both sides with clear contact paper. Now you have easy-to-clean place mats that match your wallpaper.

An old key or a large nail placed in the hem of your curtains keeps them hanging straight.

A diaper-changing table looks great later in the bathroom to hold towels and toiletries.

On a low bureau, stack four milk crates where they are two high on their ends. In the space between, slip a dowel rod or broom handle to form a clothes rod.

Make your drawers look antique by painting on a layer of white glue over the dry paint. It will dry crackly!

Use unique items for drawer handles such as beads on a string, silverware, blocks, etc.

Gut the insides of nonworking large floor stereo speakers and use as decorative boxes or for storage.

An old swing frame with the right hooks and attachments makes a good exercise equipment item.

A beat-up old dresser is great for storage in the garage or in a closet.

Buy items that have multiple uses. For example, a trunk can be used as the base for a coffee table as well as storage.

Make a kitchenette from crates or concrete blocks and various widths of shelving. You can place your smaller appliances on the shelves and use the concrete blocks for storage.

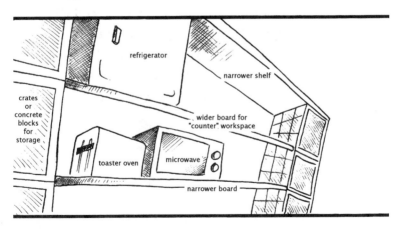

"Boards and blocks" kitchenette.

YOU KNOW YOU'RE A TIGHTWAD . . .

. . . if you thought Martha Stewart
was Jimmy Stewart's wife.

Entertaining Tightwad Style

Okay . . . . we admit it. We like to party (especially Ann). If you do, too, then let's all do it in "tightwad" style.

Tips for Any Occasion

Place a votive candle on a little melted wax inside of one half of an orange peel. The aroma will be wonderful.

Love those two- or three-tier crystal or fancy dessert dishes on a buffet table? Make your own by topping a crystal pedestal bowl with a flat crystal plate, then another pedestal bowl, etc.

Store bags of ice in your washing machine, dishwasher or bathtub when you have a bunch of company.

Orange peels in a pot of boiling water will smell like you just walked into an orange grove.

A candle placed under a cheese or vegetable grater looks great at night. Tie the top with a red ribbon.

If you have an old washer out in the garage, sell it for about $50 *or* use it for parties and reunions by adding bags of ice and placing soda cans in it.

Weddings

Use more greenery, candles, ribbon and fewer flowers in the table arrangements to save money.

When celebrating an event like a wedding or anniversary, choose a date that is close to a holiday to make use of the decorations already in place at the setting.

Add a romantic touch to any wedding or reception with simple heart-shaped decorations found anywhere.

Balloons are an economical and festive reception decoration, and can also be a good alternative to elaborate floral arrangements.

For added embellishment of the wedding cake, drape netting, lace or satin fabric on the table under the cake.

Instead of buying expensive, decorated cakes for parties, serve plainer sheet cakes.

Some shops will not charge for the groom's rental if several other outfits are rented from them. Be sure to inquire.

Look for wedding-oriented accessories at surprisingly low costs (doves, bells, etc.) as you browse through your local dollar, craft or thrift store.

Baby Showers

To make a cute silverware holder for a shower, fold a diaper into an inverted triangle. Pull up the bottom to meet the ends and then tie a white napkin with silverware to it.

Use paper cupcake holders to hold mints, etc.

Make a corsage for the mother-to-be from fancy baby socks. Group four to six socks together (depending on the size of the corsage) with a rubber band. Fluff out the sock tops to make it "flowery" and then tuck the toe and heel to the back. Add some ribbon to cover the rubber band.

Fill several decorated plastic baby bottles with jellybeans, candies, bath crystals or bath beads in pretty colors for a baby shower.

If you have a real or toy cradle (or bassinet or carriage), decorate it with ribbons and balloons. Then use it to hold the gifts before they are opened.

BRIDE'S CHECKLIST

Wedding Stationery
- ❏ Invitations
- ❏ Announcements
- ❏ Reception Cards
- ❏ Respond Cards and Envelopes
- ❏ Respond Postcards
- ❏ Informals
- ❏ At Home Cards
- ❏ Thank You Scrolls
- ❏ Thank You Notes
- ❏ Calligraphy Pens
- ❏ Wedding Programs
- ❏ Map Cards
- ❏ Pew Cards
- ❏ Calling Cards
- ❏ Photo Seals
- ❏ Bookmarks

Items for the Ceremony
- ❏ Aisle Runner
- ❏ Unity Candle
- ❏ Unity Candelabra
- ❏ Ring Bearer Pillow and Heart Tag
- ❏ Flower Girl Basket
- ❏ Taper Candles
- ❏ Bridal Purse
- ❏ Garters
- ❏ Pew Bows

Bridal Party Gifts
- ❏ Personalized Stationery
- ❏ Personalized Playing Cards
- ❏ Embroidered Gifts
- ❏ Personalized Glassware
- ❏ Appreciation Folders
- ❏ Personalized Accessories
- ❏ Specialty Gift Items

Reception Items
- ❏ Beverage, Luncheon, Dinner Napkins
- ❏ Cake Boxes or Bags
- ❏ Book and Box Matches
- ❏ Matchbook Favor Notepads
- ❏ Favor-Making Necessities
- ❏ Cake Knife and Server
- ❏ Tissue Bell Decorations
- ❏ Colored Paper Plates and Cups
- ❏ Plastic Drinkware and Flatware
- ❏ Disposable Tableware
- ❏ Disposable Ashtrays
- ❏ Thank You Ribbons and Scrolls
- ❏ Wishing Well Card Holder
- ❏ Colored Paper Streamers
- ❏ Just Married Banners and Flags
- ❏ Keepsake/Keepsake Box

BRIDE'S CHECKLIST (continued)

Reception Items (continued)

- ❏ Toasting Glasses
- ❏ Reception Aprons
- ❏ Place Cards
- ❏ Cake Top
- ❏ Klever Cards
- ❏ Table Covers
- ❏ Punch Cups
- ❏ Favor Ribbons
- ❏ Pencils
- ❏ Post-It Notes
- ❏ Plume Pen
- ❏ Candles
- ❏ Coasters
- ❏ Table Skirts
- ❏ Stir Sticks
- ❏ Balloons

Books

- ❏ Thank You Guide
- ❏ Wedding Pocket Book Planner
- ❏ Bridal Book
- ❏ Guest Book

Other Wedding Items

- ❏ Wedding File
- ❏ Bridal Gown Cover
- ❏ Personalized License Plate
- ❏ Wedding Service Video Case
- ❏ Marriage Certificate
- ❏ Car Decorating Kit
- ❏ Seeds of Love
- ❏ Bow Bag
- ❏ Gratuity Envelopes
- ❏ _____
- ❏ _____
- ❏ _____
- ❏ _____
- ❏ _____
- ❏ _____
- ❏ _____
- ❏ _____
- ❏ _____
- ❏ _____
- ❏ _____
- ❏ _____

YOU KNOW YOU'RE A TIGHTWAD . . .

. . . if your big night out begins with rolling down
the window for the tray.

Holiday Fun

R emember waiting to eat at the grown-up table or, worse yet, having to put your lanky teenage legs under the "kid" table? How about the aluminum Christmas tree? We remember it all as fun and fond memories. Here are some tips to create some memories of your own.

Scoop out a small portion of the top of some red apples, insert some green candles and add a plaid ribbon or some bells for Christmas.

Instead of pumpkin carving, just punch holes in a pattern with a large nail.

Cut out wrapping paper in various sizes of rectangles and squares. Arrange them on your front door with sticky tack to look like stacks of gift-wrapped boxes. Add sticky bows and you've got a holiday door.

Plastic Christmas tablecloths make a perfect tree skirt. Simply cut a slit in the center of the cloth and wrap around the tree.

Hang pinecones from red ribbons for a beautiful Christmas look.

Twist brown paper bags into skinny strips, about $1/2$-inch thick. Twist stripes into a wreath. Attach candy canes to the paper wreath with red pipe cleaners. Add a huge red ribbon or bow.

Cut out gingerbread men garland using brown paper bags. Attach to a Christmas ribbon and hang.

Ornaments that have broken hooks can be arranged in a glass bowl for a centerpiece.

Thread the white Styrofoam "peanuts" for a Christmas garland.

Wrap Christmas fragiles in lightbulb sleeves.

The see-through plastic deli containers from the store can be lined with tissue paper or potpourri and filled with a few little gifts. Tie closed with a big red ribbon.

For a cheap package decoration, you cannot go wrong with the ribbon that you can curl.

Wrap Christmas presents in white butcher paper or brown paper and tie with raffia or ribbon.

Wrap coffee cans in the appropriate holiday wrapping and put treats inside for guests or for family use.

Buy one nice gift for a couple, or a whole family and all the kids, for holidays or special occasions when possible.

Make a master list for Christmas and use that to organize your gifts ideas.

For holiday savings, keep your list with you all of the time. Impulsive buying or not sticking to your list will cost you more money.

A plain tan doormat becomes festive by spray-painting a Christmas tree stencil around the edges. (You can cut simple triangle stencils out of any piece of thick cardboard.)

Something as simple as an Alka-Seltzer box, wrapped in pretty paper, can make a great little house. Think about this instead of those expensive collectible houses for your Christmas scenes.

YOU KNOW YOU'RE A TIGHTWAD . . .

. . . if your husband finds his evening paper
wrapped around one of the Christmas
packages under the tree.

Kid Stuff

Our brother was seven years older than we were. After he and his friends tried to play kickball using us as the balls, our parents decided that they had better come up with some more homemade playground equipment for entertainment in the backyard.

Included in this book are tips on making everything from everyday objects that we would normally throw away. In this section you will find that you can make some really great kids' toys if you just reset your noggin' to look at objects in a different light. You will be proud of what you accomplish and set a great example for you kids about what it means to be responsible and resourceful when you practice the three Rs: reduce, reuse and recycle.

Here we are in front of the playhouse our daddy built. Hmmm . . . It looks better than some of the houses we had to live in as single moms!

Need some toy boxes? Use clothes hampers and decorate with stickers or run ribbon or material through the webbing.

A chest of drawers with a foam pad and bumper pads around the pad makes a nice changing table.

Make a child's table from a regular table by simply cutting off the legs.

An unused baby crib makes a great doll or teddy bear collection place until the crib is needed again or passed down.

Children love interesting beds. A thick foam pad and lots of fun pillows make a great floor bed. Use your imagination—add a tent!

OUR TWO CENTS

Seminars we would like to
see for husbands:

Parenting:
Beyond the Initial Conception.

Garbage:
Getting It to the Curb.

Dishwasher-Loading:
Overcoming the Fear.

You, Too, Can Fill Up an Ice Tray.

Okay, time to stop husband-bashing
(wasn't it fun, though?) and get back
to work and focus on the tips!

Save your children's old trucks, wagons, boats and even shoes for plant holders in their rooms or play yard.

Consider using primary colors in the nursery, rather than pastels. These colors can grow with a child easier.

When you need a really unique focal wall in a kids' playroom, you can buy a can of blackboard paint as a base, then let the kids go crazy with colored chalk.

Cut-outs of your children's hands with contact paper make a great ceiling border.

To keep Junior from sliding around in the high chair, trim and line the seat with a small rubber bath or sink mat.

Put a large soft towel in the bathtub to keep your toddler from slipping and sliding.

Use your leftover peel-and-stick tiles for cabinet bottoms and dollhouses.

Find a timber yard, carpenter or shop teacher, and gather their discarded blocks or wood. Simply sand off any rough or sharp edges—now you've got FREE blocks of all shapes and sizes for the kids. Use nontoxic paint or just keep au natural.

Make a car necklace from a shoestring. Tie on a penlight, a rattler, etc., depending on your child's age. (Be careful with this tip if the child is very young.)

M & M's make great game tokens for homemade board games.

Mesh laundry bags make handy bags for the beach for toys. Just shake and the sand comes out before you enter your house.

A wading pool can become a great sandbox.

A baby's hooded towel converts into a very much-used towel for the car when the children are older and have those spill "accidents."

TIGHTWAD TRUTH

It happens so quickly. The little handprints get higher and higher . . . then they disappear.

Our mama knew how to stretch a fashion dollar and give our old clothing a new look. Try some of her favorite tips to spruce up your children's wardrobes without having to go to the mall.

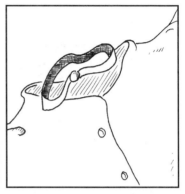

Cut out the toes of your kids' outgrown Sunday shoes to make sandals.

Make detachable white organdy collars and aprons to use on various colored homemade dresses.

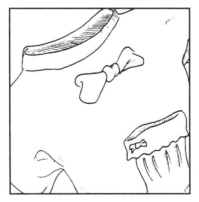

Buy white anklets and solid-colored tops
for your children add pin-on bows, flowers and
buttons to match their outfits.

Use poster board or recycled cardboard and magazine pictures to create a memory game (cut out shapes, letters, pictures, etc.).

Glue felt to the bottom of a shoe box and put felt pieces and shapes inside the box for an instant felt board game.

Make your own tape of stories for your child to listen to at night or while traveling. (Also works with regular books for adults.)

Use old business cards for flashcards. Write math problems, spelling words or other memorization items on the other side.

Traveling with a small baby? A rectangular laundry basket makes a great tote that doubles as a little crib for the hotel room. It's also a great nap bed when you're visiting someone's house.

Save that outgrown umbrella stroller for your daughter's doll stroller. This holds true for high chair and walker, too. Cut off the legs!

A pillowcase makes a great toddler costume. (Cut out holes for head and arms and add accessories for a bride, princess, Darth Vader, etc.)

Wrap several old phone books or old catalogs with duct tape and you have an instant child booster seat.

Cut two holes from the sides of a pillowcase and a hole in the middle, and you will have perfect child-sized painting smock or an apron for helping Mommy.

Use an old lunchbox to hold baby spoons, cup, bib, small box of cereal, crackers and jars of baby food. It's ready to take to Grandma's house or handy when you want to visit with a friend and the baby has to come, too.

A wooden spoon makes a great puppet. Make a face and dress it up.

Make a shoebox dollhouse. Use the lids for roof and staple together the boxes into any plan you want.

Detergent scoop toy.

Believe it or not, detergent scoops make great toys! Tie one end of a string to its handle, and the other end to a small object such as a tiny car, a paper clip, a key, etc. Kids love trying to catch the object in the scoop—and the longer the string, the harder it is to catch!

Cover a child's dresser drawers in comic strip paper. Cover the paper with a coat of white glue and water.

An old towel can be cut to make a bib. Make a slit for the head.

OUR TWO CENTS

We read a research report that said all of your childrearing answers can be found in a book.
That author never had a child with beans up his nose!

Make a bib by cutting a circle from an old sweatshirt using the hole as the center.

Create a train for your child with shoe boxes and shoestrings.

Place a ball onto a skinny wood dowel, about one-quarter inch thick, first adding a plastic cup in the middle, and cover with old knee sock decorated with a funny face. It becomes a cute pop-up toy.

Blue jean pockets become an instant little carrier—add a shoestring for the handle. Write the child's name on it in black marker. Decorate as desired. We call these "Pocket Pals" and can be great to use in restaurants stuffed with goodies.

TIGHTWAD TRUTH

Some people say that the hardest part of being a mother is the labor and delivery part. Those people never had to watch their baby go to kindergarten on his or her first day of school.

Cookie sheets can be painted with non-toxic spray paint and make excellent lap trays for kids in the car. Use several light coats, allowing each to dry completely before applying the next.

> ## OUR TWO CENTS
> Somebody said that a mother is an unskilled laborer . . . that somebody probably never gave a bath to a squirmy baby.

Orphaned gloves become mini puppets with a little imagination. Decorate orphaned socks for puppets or holiday stockings.

A Styrofoam egg carton is a neat twelve-color paint palette for a child. Simply close to keep the colors liquid.

Save milk jugs and cut out the sides to form a handled scoop. Make two and throw a ball back and forth with the kids.

Wrap a gift for a child with comic strips.

Use stickers to decorate kids' gifts.

Wrap a teenager's gift with the newspaper sports page or the fashion page.

The tops of your yogurt containers or butter tubs are great "wheels" for a wagon you can make from a shoebox and a shoestring. Put on with brads.

Save your macaroni and cheese boxes, shoe boxes, detergent boxes, etc. Cover in contact paper or material, and use as building blocks for your children. Stuff them with paper before you cover or tape them.

Oh, the joy of a cardboard box—make a handle from a shoestring to pull it like a wagon and add more boxes to form a toy train.

Shoe boxes stacked and stapled or taped together form an instant dollhouse. Cut out pictures of clocks, rugs, pictures, even wallpaper, from J. C. Penny or other store catalogs!

A huge box is a huge playhouse!

An old broomstick and two chairs for end supports make a great limbo game.

Empty liter bottles are quite entertaining. For instance, they make great bowling pins for indoor or outside. Or cut out the bottoms, turn upside down and stick the spout into the ground—ready for a game of ball toss?

Find duplicate objects such as two clock pictures and tape onto cards and make a memory game.

Save that wading pool with a crack in it to kick under the bed for instant toy storage.

Here we go with the box again—draw a clown face with a huge hole for a mouth and toss in a sponge or beanbag.

Make plastic rings out of the tops of containers like Cool Whip by cutting out the middles. Stick an old broomstick in the ground for a game of ring toss.

Make an obstacle course with old tires.

Laundry baskets: Add a shoestring for a wagon or tack to the wall for a ball toss. They make great toy boxes too!

Make a Nerf ball from about two or three sponges—stack them and secure with a rubber band, then twist into a roundish shape.

A clean paintbrush and a bowl or bucket of water makes a great outside activity. Kids love to paint, and water will not make such a mess.

Water-filled spray bottles are great for outside play. Put on an old T-shirt and squirt! For extra fun, put in food coloring—perhaps blue for one player and red for another. After a time limit, the one with the most color on his or her shirt loses!

Here is an example of our daddy's handiwork on Christmas morning. Notice the homemade cradles and the chalkboard, which we have to this day. (Our daddy is now eighty-six).

Build your child's own fun playground. Use old tires, painted barrels, beams, anything you can think of! We hung a large toy bucket from a pivot hook and chain and a beam and it spins! Remember to make sure that all equipment is free of sharp edges and can hold the appropriate weight. Be sure to use lumber that is not treated with toxic chemicals and recessed bolts.

Make your teenager a snoozing shirt from Daddy's old shirt. Choose a white one and decorate with painted-on ZZZ's.

Use a milk crate for a toddler swing—cut out holes for the legs, smoothing the edges with sandpaper or duct tape, and hang securely by a rope or chain.

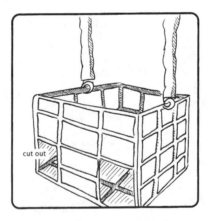

Cut out leg holes in a plastic crate for a toddler swing (sand down sharp plastic edges).

Make a double stroller by connecting two umbrella strollers together. Use Velcro strips to attach.

Save your crib sheets and use them to temporarily slipcover your car's backseat when you are traveling with little ones or pets.

An old bookcase is great to make a dollhouse.

Don't buy expensive dollhouses; make one yourself from a bookshelf! Add doors, a roof, and make it as tall and as big as the bookshelf you have chosen.

This is really a money-saver! Buy lots of solid white, tan or black T-shirts for your small children. They will match anything that they have in the closet.

The hand-me-down boy clothes that your little girl has inherited can be made into little girl clothes by adding tied ribbons or girlish buttons. Do this also to plain white socks.

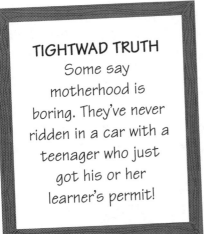

TIGHTWAD TRUTH
Some say
motherhood is
boring. They've never
ridden in a car with a
teenager who just
got his or her
learner's permit!

Designate one place (and no more) for jackets, school notes, school bags, etc.

The memory trick of learning test facts is priceless. (Italy looks like an Italian boot, Chile is shaped like a long chili pepper.)

Keep three boxes in the bottom of every child's closet (yours, too!): Store (memory items and certificates), Sell and Share (give away). We call these the "3 S's" of organization.

Label your kids' dresser drawers so that they can put clothes away on laundry day.

Label drawers for your children so that they can put away their own clothes as well as find them easily.

When cleaning up baby, use one color wash cloth for goo on the face and another color for the other end. It's best not to get the colors mixed up. Even though you wash them all, it's best keep them separate when laundering and to use bleach for the bottom-cleaning cloths.

Try using dark-colored hand towels for the kiddies to keep stains to a minimum.

Make sure the kids have their homework done and that it's with their coat or jacket by the front door. Do they need money for lunch or whatever? Put it with the jacket and homework. Now!

If your children take their lunch to school, pack it the night before and put it in the refrigerator.

Buy or make pillow shams instead of using regular pillow-cases in a kid's room. Decorative side up for daytime, flip it for bedtime. We call this the "flip-flop" pillow.

Funky Craft Dough You Can Eat

1 cup butter or margarine, softened
6 hard-cooked egg yolks, mashed
2 tsps. cream of tarter
5 cups all-purpose flour
1 cup shortening

2 $\frac{1}{2}$ cups sifted powdered sugar
2 tsps. baking soda
1 tbsp. vanilla extract
Red, yellow, green paste food coloring

Cream butter and shortening; add sugar, beating until light and fluffy. Add the egg yolks, soda, cream of tarter, and vanilla, beating well. Add flour a little at a time, mixing well. Divide the dough into 4 equal parts. Color one part red, one yellow, one green, and leave the last dough part plain. Wrap each part up separately in plastic wrap and chill at least 1 hour.

Here's the part the children love! They can hand-shape the dough into anything they want, or roll out the dough and cut it with cookie cutters. Bake their creations at 350 degrees for 8 to 10 minutes. Let the cookies cool on the baking sheet for a few minutes.

Play Dough: Mix 2 cups flour, 1 cup salt, $\frac{1}{2}$ cup cornstarch, $1\frac{1}{4}$ tablespoons baking soda, 2 cups water, 1 tablespoon cooking oil and a pinch of food coloring; microwave for about 4 minutes on high and store in an air-tight plastic container.

No-Cook Play Dough: 1 cup flour, $\frac{1}{4}$ cup salt and $\frac{3}{8}$ cup hot water from your faucet; add food coloring if you desire.

Gooey Slime: 8 oz. white glue, $\frac{3}{4}$ cup water, 1 teaspoon 20 Mule Team borax (boy, does this bring back memories for us); add food coloring if you desire.

Silly Willy Putty: 8 oz. white glue, 2 teaspoons 20 Mule Team borax and 3 teaspoons water.

CHILD IMMUNIZATION RECORD

Name: _____

Birth date: _____

Type of Shot	Dose #	Needed at:	Date given:
OPV (oral polio vaccine)	1st	2 months	_____
	2nd	4 months	_____
	3rd	15 months	_____
	4th	Before school	_____
DPT (diptheria-pertussis-tetanus)	1st	2 months	_____
	2nd	4 months	_____
	3rd	6 months	_____
	4th	15 months	_____
	5th	Before starting school	_____
	Adult Booster	Every 10 years (diptheria and tetanus)	_____
MMR (measles-mumps-rubella)	1st	15 months	_____
	2nd	Before starting school	_____
Hib (bacterial meningitis)	1st	2 months	_____
	2nd	4 months	_____
	3rd	6 months	_____
	4th	15 months	_____
HBV (hepatitis B virus)	1st	At birth	_____
	2nd	1–2 months	_____
	3rd	6–18 months	_____

Notes: _____

_____

BABY PLANNING

Before you even think about a baby!

☐ Review health insurance coverage BEFORE conception.

☐ If necessary, buy health insurance, paying special attention to the date when your pregnancy will be covered. (Could save you thousands!)

AFTER CONCEPTION:

First Month

☐ Select a doctor. Get recommendations. Check credentials. Interview prospective doctors or midwifes. Find out where your prospective healthcare professionals have staff privileges. Make your selection.

☐ Decide where to have your baby: a hospital? a birth center? at home?

☐ Visit the facilities if the location of where you would like to deliver plays a major role in determining who will deliver your baby.

☐ Select a facility.

☐ Again, consult with the insurance company to clarify which specific procedures during pregnancy are covered.

Fourth Month

☐ Review the maternity/paternity policy at your workplace(s).

Fifth Month

☐ Plan your will. Estimate your net worth. Plan the distribution of your assets. Make an appointment with an attorney. Select an executor and get his or her approval.

Fifth Month (*continued*)

☐ Select guardians. Select a guardian of the person and a guardian of the estate. Make sure the guardian is willing to serve.

☐ Assess your life insurance needs. Estimate the amount you will need. Decide what kind of policy you will need.

Sixth Month

☐ Make your will. Meet with an attorney. Draft a power of attorney. Draft a living will. Write a letter of final instructions.

☐ Inform your guardian of your child-rearing wishes. Write a letter of parental guidance.

☐ Evaluate insurance options. Collect estimates from four or five life insurance companies.

Seventh Month

☐ Execute your will. Complete your will. Store it in a safe place.

☐ Buy life insurance. Purchase the best of policies you have reviewed. Store the policy in a safe place.

☐ Prepare for your hospital stay. Take childbirth classes. Review your insurance coverage to make sure you understand the coverage and procedures. Estimate your out-of-pocket health-care expenses.

☐ Prepare for the homecoming. Arrange for childcare for other children, if any. Buy or borrow furniture and equipment. Interview pediatricians. Ask other mothers.

Eight Month

☐ Prepare for your hospital stay. Preregister at the hospital. Notify your insurance company and get a precertification number, if necessary.

Ninth Month

☐ Enjoy your last month of great sleep for a long, long while.

YOU KNOW YOU'RE A TIGHTWAD . . .

. . . if your children discover in first grade that
crayons have paper around them!

PART
THREE

TURNING TRASH INTO CASH: Million-Dollar Tips That Will Change Your Financial Life Forever

Money Talks

We're not called the Tightwad Twins for nothin'. In this section, you will find everything from Freebie offers to advice on financial aid and mortgages, to tables and checklists to help you budget. We've also included some ideas for how to earn fast cash, as well as some cost-conscious tips on reusing common items like envelopes and Christmas cards. This section is about saving pennies to saving thousands.

COMMON CENTS

Funny how a $10 bill looks so big when you put it in the church offering, but so small when you take it to the market!

Money-Savers for the Tightwad Family

To find a qualified real estate appraiser, contact the Appraisal Institute at (312) 335-4100.

For a back issue of *Consumer Reports* annual auto buyer's guide, send $5.00 to *Consumer Reports,* P.O. Box 2015, Yonkers, NY 10703.

Free credit help is available from National Foundation for Consumer Credit, call (800) 388-2227.

To get your copy of IRS Publication 587, The Business Use of Your Home, call (800) 829-1040.

To find scholarship money for college, use the Internet (*www.fastweb.com*). They list 180,000 private scholarships!

For scholarships and grants, call the National Scholarship Research Service at (707) 545-5777 *(24-hour message center)*

American Association of Retired Persons
1-800-424-2277

For credit reports ($8 per individual; $16 joint),
call these numbers:

Equifax 1-800-685-1111

Experience Credit Data 1-800-682-7654

Trans Union 1-800-851-2674

For child support help, order the free Enforcement at National Reference Center, OCSE, 370 L'Enfant Promenade, S.W., Washington, DC 20447.

Pell Grants are grants of $200 to $2,100 per year, based on financial need and academic achievement. Look for the federal government's Free Application for Student Federal Aid (FASFA) in any college office.

Supplemental Education opportunity grants are grants from $200 to $400 per year, based on need. To apply, a student should request information directly from the financial aid offices of the college he or she will attend.

A PENNY FOR YOUR THOUGHTS

A reader sent this ad in to show us that marriage CAN be profitable!
FOR SALE BY OWNER
Complete set of encyclopedias. Forty-five volumes. $1,000 or best offer. No longer needed. Got married last weekend and wife knows everything.

The Consumer Information Catalog is a list of more than two hundred booklets filled with priceless information on topics such as cars, children, parenting, employment, environment, government programs, food, benefits, medical problems, housing tips, home improvements, money problems, credit problems, financial planning, small businesses, travel, hobbies, human rights and assistance programs. Most booklets are free, some are 50 cents to $2.00—write to this address and ask for a CIC (Consumer Information Catalog):

Catalog Department
Consumer Information Center-6D
P.O. Box 100
Pueblo, CO 81002
.... or fax this request to (719) 948-9724
.... or use the Internet at *http://www.pueblo.gsa.gov*

For 5 Financial Aid Programs (Publication 522Y) contact:
Consumer Information Center
Department 522Y
Pueblo, CO 81009
(719) 948-3334

You can get a 119-page booklet that provides information on over one hundred housing programs offered by HUD. Call 1-202-708-1420 and ask for the booklet "Programs of HUD."

Home by Choice is a national network of Christian mothers who have chosen to stay home with their young children. Many of them work part time from home. Their Newsletter, *Table Talk* is bimonthly and costs $15 annually; it can be used as a limited networking source. P.O. Box 103, Vienna, VA 22183.

Mother's Home Business Network offers several manuals, a newsletter called *Homeworking Mothers,* and networking opportunities with other members. Membership is $19. To sign up, call (516) 997-7394.

Mother and Home books offer a rich selection of how-to books and books for inspiration on very specific work-at-home topics such as running a mail-order business. (801) 457-1993.

The Whole Work Catalog offers a broad spectrum of books and other resources on alternative work styles. Ask for a copy by calling (303) 447-1087.

General Tips for the Tightwad Family

Write product manufacturers and ask for coupons. You might be surprised to find coupons from some of them waiting for you in your mailbox.

If your child has a B average in school, you are entitled to a car insurance discount. This applies also if your child has had any driving education.

Reuse window envelopes that come in your mail.

Send Christmas postcards for 20 cents instead of a card that carries the full price of a stamp.

Keeping your trunk empty and your tires properly inflated helps to save gas.

Don't panic about college financing if you didn't start saving early— the financial aid packages are great. Simply walk into the financial aid office of the college, and they will help you find a creative way to finance an education.

> **COMMON CENTS**
> Wealth does not lie in the extent of your possessions but in the fewness of your wants.

You can spend six to ten dollars a day for lunch and snacks. That is close to three hundred dollars per month! Instead, eat last night's leftovers or buy cheaper lunch items when you grocery shop.

Don't be intimidated by impatient grocery cashiers when they see you coming with your coupons. It's your money you are saving, not theirs!

Find a table or nice chair or a chest in the alley put out on trash day? Put it in your trunk and place it in your front yard with a bright sign of $5 or $10 on it. You WILL sell it!

Put all of your change in a jar at the end of the day. Take it to a change counter that some grocery stores offer.

You must do this! Change the number of exemptions on your withholding form at work to less dependents. More tax will be withheld from each paycheck, but you will get a better tax refund. (Yes, we know, you could be putting the difference in a savings account and make better interest. But would you really *do* it? We like the KISS rule on savings: keep it super simple.)

Sign up for a payroll savings plan. You will not miss the money because you never see it. It's almost painless.

When it comes to creating a resume: Fit in, but stand out. For example, end your resume with a personal

COMMON CENTS
Be thankful for taxes. They mean you have income.

statement of commitment to be the best employee possible. Also, "sell" yourself. Be enthusiastic and motivated. Make the presentation of your resume stand out, too: use color, graphics or interesting paper stock if appropriate.

Working your way out of a debt hole? Motivate yourself by making a colorful chart just like you did as a child, checking off the payments made as you make them. On the chart, make a place for total payments also. Example: twenty more car payments—make twenty little car squares and mark off one at a time. You get the picture.

Run to the dumpsters at the end of each semester at your local college—the throw-aways are unbelievable!

Obtain six to eight weeks of free credit by buying just after the billing date and paying in full just before the due date.

Ask about special government financing rates to new home-owners. There are programs you would not believe for first-time buyers. Just ask a real estate agent!

If you are experiencing credit problems, try to work with a consumer credit counselor before taking the drastic step of filing bankruptcy. They're in the phone book—and they're free! Just be careful about who you choose since there are also many unscrupulous credit counselors in business. Contact your local chamber of commerce or Better Business Bureau for a referral.

Don't take out a home equity loan unless you're one of those strong people who never borrows for the wrong reasons.

You may benefit from mortgage refinancing if you can obtain a rate at least 1.5 percent less that your present mortgage rate.

Before beginning your home search, find out how much home you can afford to buy by speaking with a lender.

TIGHTWAD TRUTH

Why can't we put our helpless husbands down as a child-care deduction or deduct $5 for every mosquito bite acquired on a Scout trip? And what is wrong with deducting the gas you use going to sales or to the non-stop flow of school functions? How about deducting one semester of tuition for your child for every hour of intense labor while giving birth? Now, that's fair! Or even all the money spent on chocolate since it does act as an antidepressant. And finally, why can't we deduct fifty dollars for every single "A" our kids make on report cards (because behind every good student is a mother who sat up until two in the morning coloring a map of China!).

Apply for a loan first at your credit union. Credit unions often have lower interest rates than savings and loans and banks.

Take the time to learn every detail about your company's insurance plan.

> ## A PENNY FOR YOUR THOUGHTS
>
> "Save your riches and store them in heaven, where moths and rust cannot destroy nor robbers steal . . . your heart lies where your riches are."
>
> —Matthew 6:19–21

Figure out the minimum amount of life insurance you need by adding up all of your debts and adding about 10 percent extra for living expenses. You will want to cover your debts *and* have some left over.

YOU KNOW YOU'RE A TIGHTWAD . . .

. . . if you thought that you could declare your helpless husband as a child-care deduction.

AMORTIZATION TABLE

The table below will assist you in determining the monthly Principal & Interest Payment for a loan amount. Simply divide your mortgage amount by $1,000 and multiply by the factor below.

Note: You will need an approximate interest rate and a loan amount.

Amortization Table

Term/Rate	10 year	15 year	20 year	25 year	30 year
5	10.61	7.91	6.60	5.85	5.37
5.25	10.73	8.04	6.74	6.00	5.53
5.5	10.86	8.18	6.88	6.15	5.68
5.75	10.98	8.31	7.03	6.30	5.84
6	11.11	8.44	7.17	6.45	6.00
6.25	11.23	8.58	7.31	6.60	6.16
6.5	11.36	8.72	7.46	6.76	6.33
6.75	11.49	8.85	7.61	6.91	6.49
7	11.62	8.99	7.76	7.07	6.66
7.25	11.75	9.13	7.91	7.23	6.83
7.5	11.88	9.28	8.06	7.39	7.00
7.75	12.01	9.42	8.21	7.56	7.17
8	12.14	9.56	8.37	7.72	7.34
8.25	12.27	9.71	8.53	7.89	7.52
8.5	12.40	9.85	8.68	8.06	7.69
8.75	12.54	10.00	8.84	8.23	7.87
9	12.67	10.15	9.00	8.40	8.05
9.25	12.81	10.30	9.16	8.57	8.23
9.5	12.94	10.45	9.33	8.74	8.41
9.75	13.08	10.60	9.49	8.92	8.60

DETAILED BUDGET

Expenses	Budgeted Expense	Actual Expense
Housing		
Rent or Mortgage	$	$
Real estate taxes	$	$
Homeowner's insurance	$	$
Water	$	$
Heat	$	$
Electricity	$	$
Gas	$	$
Telephone	$	$
Food		
Groceries	$	$
Restaurants	$	$
Clothing/Shoes		
Husband	$	$
Wife	$	$
Child	$	$
Child	$	$

Expenses	Budgeted Expense	Actual Expense
Household/Yard		
Laundry	$	$
Dry cleaning	$	$
Repair	$	$
Housekeeping	$	$
Gardening	$	$
Medical		
Doctor	$	$
Dentist	$	$
Prescriptions	$	$
Over-the-counter drugs	$	$
Insurance payments	$	$
Child Care		
Daycare	$	$
Baby-sitters	$	$

DETAILED BUDGET (continued)

Expenses	Budgeted Expense	Actual Expense	Expenses	Budgeted Expense	Actual Expense
Child Supplies			**Transportation**		
Toys and games	$	$	Taxi	$	$
Lessons & instructions	$	$	Carpool	$	$
Diapers, etc.	$	$	Parking	$	$
Extracurricular school fees	$	$	**Miscellaneous**		
			Newspapers		
Auto			Magazines		
Loan payments	$	$	Organization dues	$	$
Insurance	$	$	Toiletries	$	$
Maintenance	$	$	Hobby supplies	$	$
Repair	$	$	Music	$	$
			Books	$	$
Gas and Oil			**Gifts/Other**		
Household Equipment					
Appliances	$	$		$	$
Furniture	$	$		$	$
Tools	$	$		$	$

DEBTS

Loan Type	Lender	Amount of Loan	Interest Rate	Balance Due	Monthly Payment
Car loan:		$	____%	$	$
Education loan:		$	____%	$	$
Home improvement:		$	____%	$	$

Mortgage

Mortgage holder:		$	____%	$	$
Mortgage balance:		$	____%	$	$
Interest rate:		$	____%	$	$
Monthly payments:		$	____%	$	$

CREDIT CARDS

Name of Card	Account Number	Balance Due
1.		$
2.		$
3.		$
4.		$
5.		$

PERSONAL CONTACTS

Name	Address	Phone	Fax
Accountant:			
Attorney:			
Banker:			
Clergyman:			
Executor of estate:			
Friend:			

Insurance Agents

Auto:			
Disability:			
Homeowner's:			
Life:			
Medical:			
Other:			
Neighbor:			
Next of kin:			
Physician:			
Work contact:			

LAST WILL AND TESTAMENT

of

_____

I, _____, of _____,

in the County of _____ and State of _____,
do hereby revoke any and all wills and testamentary dispositions heretofore
made by me and hereby make, publish and declare this as and for my Last
Will and Testament.

FIRST: I nominate and appoint _____, of _____
as the executor of this my Last Will and Testament. I direct that
no bond or other security shall be required of my said executor
for the faithful performance of his or her duties in any jurisdic-
tion in which he or she may be called upon to act.

I nominate and appoint _____, of _____
as the guardian of the person of my minor children if I should die
as the role of parent of such minor children. If _____
shall predecease me, fail to qualify or cease to act as such
guardian for any reason, I nominate and appoint _____
_____, of _____, as successor
guardian. Any guardian so appointed shall be exempt from giving
bond or other security.

SECOND: I direct that all of my just debts and funeral expenses be paid as
soon after my death as shall be practicable.
I direct my executor to pay from my residuary estate all admin-
istrative expenses and death taxes imposed on my estate.

THIRD: I give, devise, and bequeath my property as follows:

IN WITNESS WHEREOF, I have hereunto set my hand and seal this _____
day of _____, signed, sealed, published and declared
by _____, the testator therein named, as and
for the Testator's Last Will and Testament in the presence of us, and we, at
the Testator's request and in his/her presence and in the presence of each
other, have signed our names as witnesses thereto.

LAST WILL AND TESTAMENT *(continued)*

_____ residing at _____

_____

_____

_____ residing at _____

_____

_____

_____ residing at _____

_____

_____

GENERAL POWER OF ATTORNEY

BE IT KNOWN THAT, _____ has made and

appointed, and by these presents does make and appoint _____

_____ true and lawful attorney for him/her and in his/her

name, place and stead, giving and granting to said attorney, general, full

and unlimited power and authority to do and perform all and every act and

thing whatsoever requisite necessary to be done in and about the prem-

ises as fully, to all intents and purposes, as could be done if personally

present, with full power of substitution and revocation, hereby ratifying

and confirming all that said attorney shall lawfully do or cause to be done

by virtue hereof.

Signed this date: _____

Signature must be notarized

Witnessed by Notary

YOU KNOW YOU'RE A TIGHTWAD . . .

. . . if you've ever signed a petition to have the National Anthem words changed to "Buy One, Get One Free."

In this section, we give you really big tips that we have both used and still use today. You can actually change your financial life! All it takes is an open mind and a determination not to listen to others' opinions as to why you need to do this—if these tips are right for your family financially, then do them! Follow them faithfully and you will succeed at cutting down your expenses DRASTICALLY!

Yes, God can move mountains, but he expects us to do a little work too! In our society, it is nearly impossible for a couple to buy a house without borrowing and that's only if you can get past the huge cash down payment! Are there ways to do this? Yes, there are a few, but as with anything worth having there is a little research, effort, and mortgage moving prayer to go with it. Here are some of the ways you can buy a house with no down payment. Later, we'll show you how to NOT make the mortgage payment after you get it! Makes no sense? It will: Read on to find your dream house.

> ### A TIGHTWAD TRUTH
> Keep track of small expenses; a small leak can sink a big ship!

> ### COMMON CENTS
> God gives every bird its food, but he does not throw it into its nest!

Appraisal Value

Don't let this fancy word scare you: It can be your free ticket to buying a home WITHOUT A DOWN PAYMENT. Simply, you are looking for a house that is selling below its appraised value. How will you know it? Do you order appraisals for every house on the market? Of course not, but what you do is look for houses in the newspapers, on the Web, or in neighborhoods that seem to be selling for less than you expected or lower than the rest of the neighborhood. Now comes the clincher: Ask yourself why is this house selling so low? It could be the street has gotten a lot busier over the years and people are trying to sell and get out; or it could be the house needs some TLC; or it could be just that the house has fourteen bedrooms and only one bathroom!

Whatever the reason, if you can live with the problems then you have a chance to buy it. How? A new trend is happening in the lending world and has finally affected the big banks' thinking also: the idea of creative financing. What's even more exciting is there are real estate agents who will stick with you and help you get a look at these houses. Be upfront with all of them: You do not have a cash down payment but you do have a steady job and good credit if they care. Tell them you are looking for houses selling under appraised value only!

So who pays the down payment? The lending institution does now and you do later—it is all counted into the total cost of the house. And if you find your dream home and must have it, then offer to pay them a little more than their asking price (to be totaled into the house's total selling price), and they will probably pay the closing costs (if they have not offered already to do so anyway) and any other expenses.

The drawback is only that you may have to live with a noisy street or less bathrooms or paint the house yourself. You may or may not end up paying more than the selling price, but this is a good way to get into a home. The other alternative, remember, is to pay rent for years while trying to save up thousands and having no equity—not much of a choice.

Contract to Deed (Rent to Own)

Granted you don't find many homes with this option, but you have to know what to look for. Is there a house that has been on the market forever and it is not selling? Perhaps at

this time they are just wanting someone to simply sign a financial legal agreement that the house deed will be delivered when so many payments have been made for so many years. This will help the sellers to move on to another place if they desire just the sale without cash money from their home: They are freed from the obligation, and they still get their equity back that they have paid, just in payments.

This idea can also be done for mobile homes, which we encourage buying rather than renting an apartment. Yes, we know mobile homes go down in value instead of up, but this mobile home can be your rental property later. If you put the mobile home on land, you can use this property later, after it is paid for, as a down payment to build a house in front of your mobile home and then have that payment made by renting the mobile home! Be sure to put the mobile home on the very back of your property if you have plans to build. A word of caution on using the contract to deed method: This is not the same as leasing a house with an option to buy. Leasing with an option to buy usually entails only a part of your rent money going to purchase the house and then some upfront money after a couple of years or so. Go with the contract to deed for a set amount of years and set amount of payments. We have included a sample copy of a contract to deed or rent to own agreement in our time management chapter. However, you need to take the advice of an attorney or at least have a paralegal draw up a contract for you—the sellers will probably want to do this, too! Let them. It will save you money, and you can still pay less by allowing an attorney to check it out. Always make sure any legal document is filed at your courthouse. This is a must! Sometimes, the seller will even pay the filing fee.

So now you have a house. Now what's this about not making a mortgage payment? Read on. . . .

OUR TWO CENTS
WANTED:
A house that earns
its own mortgage
payment!

Making Money While You Sleep

Our parents were true tightwads: They made only a few mortgage payments in their lifetime thanks to their God-given gift of imagination and creativity. Daddy turned an extra bedroom and a bathroom into an apartment, and he did it with no construction costs! First he put the existing tall window on hinges to make an outside entrance. Then he formed a mini-kitchen in the bathroom using stacked concrete blocks and boards, painted a nice color of course, and for a countertop he used floor tiles! (We have even used peel-and-stick tile). He added a salvage yard refrigerator (today you can buy a small one for under $100) and a hot plate (plus a microwave today). Our mama offered free laundry service one day a week to the renter, utilities were paid, and she also cleaned the tiny apartment once a week (we do not do this for our tenants, but you could offer that option). So for the price of rent, the tenant got free maid service, free laundry service, no utilities, and a quiet place in a wonderful home—the home of the Tightwad Twins who were only babies then! So remember, any bedroom with a bathroom can be an efficiency apartment using our daddy's "boards and blocks" kitchen or by simply putting a tiny refrigerator and microwave in the bathroom next to the sink)! Remember, your tenant does not have to be your roommate. We were not even aware that someone else lived in our family's home upstairs until we were in the seventh grade!

This is called "making money while you sleep!"

Before we leave this tip, we need to give you some advice we have learned:

> **COMMON CENTS**
> Women are the CEOs of running their home . . . is your home financially profitable or always "in the red"?

1. Check out the tenant's criminal background.
2. Call their last landlord as well as all of their job and personal references.
3. Do not tell others in the neighborhood that you are renting an apartment. Use the word roommate if anyone asks.

4. Do NOT have a written lease. Have a verbal agreement only, because your tenant may not pay the rent one month and then you can simply put their stuff out on the curb. If they try to legally make a problem or call the police, you can simply plead your case that this person is a squatter and they do not have a written lease agreement! With a lease, you have to go through the eviction process which can take up to three months or more—three months that you will lose in rent money! We do recommend that your tenant sign a statement for YOUR RECORDS ONLY that says " I, _____, the tenant at _____ address, sign this statement that I will not hold the owners of this address responsible for any fires, thefts, or injuries, regardless of the circumstances. I also understand that my deposit of $_____ is nonrefundable when I leave." Do NOT give them a copy of this agreement or allow them to copy it or keep it.

5. Ask for a modest deposit only. This can cover any damages done to the apartment when the tenant leaves. Just be sure to add the line above concerning the deposit.

6. Try to rent to someone you know, but if you can't, run an ad in your neighborhood newspaper. Here is a sample of one we have used successfully:

    "Small, but clean, efficiency apartment in a family home. Private entrance, small outside sitting area, $____ deposit required. Must have clean criminal background, good landlord references, job references and personal references. No pets or children. Free utilities, free phone (get a teenager ring number), *free cable* (run

a line connector from your main cable with a splicer).
Call _____." (using the word "free" is enticing).

Here are some examples of how two creative women put
their houses to work and made money while they slept!

3 BEDROOM/2 BATH TOWNHOME

As you can see, by simply closing off some hallway doors and cutting
some doors, this single woman who does not need the other two bedrooms
or bath and can live mortgage free!

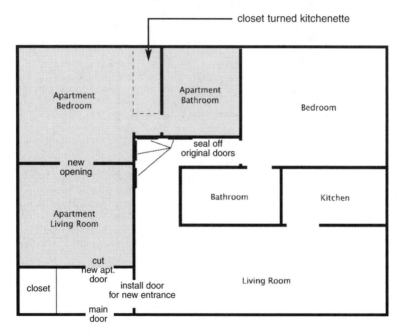

MOBILE HOME

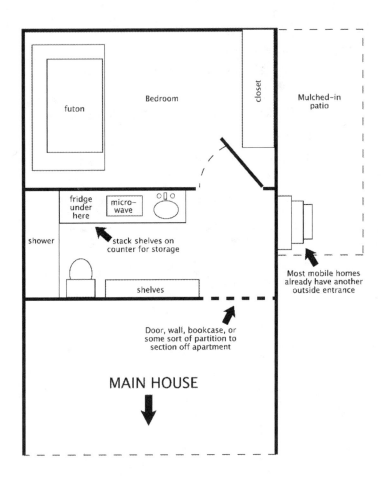

Almost everyone struggles financially at one time or another, but these can be overcome with a smart strategy. Remember Moses? He had to worry about that large group of people in the desert. He had to feed them—all three million of them! According to a well-known army general, Moses would have had to have fifteen hundred tons of food a day or about two full freight trains, each a mile long. In the desert alone, they would have needed about four thousand tons of wood a day to cook or stay warm at night just for one day. And what about water? They had no lakes, only a few wells. They needed about one million gallons a day! Every time they camped, they needed a space the size of Rhode Island or 750 square miles! The trip across the Red Sea had to be done in one day so that means they had to tread fast, and even if they formed a double line eight hundred miles long, it would take them thirty-five days to do so. How did he do it? Of course, we know it was a miracle from God, but we can still draw on the part that you need to have faith in yourself that you can get your mortgage paid or conquer another financial hardship. Remember Moses—and we don't even want to think about Noah and all of those animals!

"Is Your Second Income Working for You or Are You Working for It?"

Okay, before you hate us, let us emphasize this: We do not condemn the mom who is married and works, but only offer tips to help her cope better with time and money problems. However, for the married mom who wants to consider the option to stay home (we know the single mom simply cannot

COMMON CENTS

Try to buy a home that is a two-family dwelling or at least has three or four bedrooms, one with a bathroom that can easily be converted to form an efficiency apartment. Look at the floor plan. Can a simple wall be put up in a hallway as a divider or a large window that can be converted to an outside door, or is one of the bedrooms isolated with a bathroom that the rest of the family does not need? Be imaginative! If you get discouraged, think of the Tightwad Twins. Someone else has been making our mortgage payments for years . . . even now!

quit), then we offer this test to evaluate whether this is a viable possibility. This may be more applicable for moms of pre-school children, but it can work for families with older children, too. We saw a segment on "Dateline" whereby a couple was shocked to see where their money was going, and the wife actually cried because she had been working and putting the kids in daycare, all for expenses that they could have easily eliminated. She quit the next day!

The Test:

Add up all the expenses you have each month by working: second car, parking, lunches, tolls, gas, clothes, daycare, or sitter/housecleaner, and any other expense, no matter how small. Label this column "work expenses." Now, deduct this amount from your net pay per month. Label this amount YOUR REAL NET PAY. Next deduct your paycheck net pay from your REAL NET pay. If they are even, then you are literally working for no profit. If there is still a profit showing because you are working, then go one step further. Deduct from that profit any expenses that you have now AND DID NOT INCLUDE ON THE WORKING LIST OF EXPENSES. For example, can you learn to cut the kids' hair, eliminate the second car completely and have your husband ride in a carpool or train, cook more from scratch? Anything that you can save money on because you will be home. Now, the question: IS YOUR SECOND INCOME WORKING FOR YOU, OR ARE YOU WORKING FOR IT? Is it worth you working and putting the kids in daycare or with someone other than their mother? Even if you bite the budget bullet only for the preschool years, it is an option you might want to consider. Don't forget to carefully read the chapter on our really big financial tips. You can save even more. For example, the "making money while you sleep" tip could eliminate your mortgage payment! Get going. If you want to stay home with your children, then you have to do your homework!

If you're a mom and become discouraged, just remember that God had trouble with His children, too. His first word to them was "Don't." We all know how that went.

Guaranteed Fast-Cash Businesses

Let's get right to the point. There are many ways to make cash. However, if you choose only one way that is right for you, then you can succeed. We want to remind you once again to refer to the big tip concerning the efficiency apartment idea: It is BIG cash and you can make it while you sleep! Some of these cash businesses will sound absurd to some of you, however, it may be just the right job for another. You can do these jobs by word of mouth, by a simple ad, or by making some business cards that are unique and spreading them around. Now, let's make some money!

1. Offer to be a paid companion to an older person. Run errands for the elderly or clean and cook for them.
2. Call a marketing research company and ask to be put on their lists.
3. Be a homework tutor. One child, every day, can be a regular cash business. You can even arrange to pick up the child from school, offer a snack, and keep the child until his or her mom picks the child up from work. Pass out flyers at school to moms or run an ad. You're a mom, for Pete's sake. You do not have to have a degree to do this. No one has more experience in this than a mother!
4. Selling information is so easy and profitable. A Web site can do wonders for your pocketbook. We sold information packets on various money solutions on our Web site and linked it to other busy Web sites so that their traffic they could see our Web site button. It is easy cash money. We have no idea how to create a Web site. However, in today's world, even teenagers can make one, so seek

them out. Another way is to place an ad for your information. Do you like to cook and have unusual recipes or do you have a newsletter that can sell? How about a craft item or even the instructions to an unusual craft?

5. An Eternal Yard Sale is our favorite! If you have a garage, then you can have a little business. An Eternal Yard Sale means that you can have many yard sales with little planning. How? All it takes are really good signs positioned at intersections, leading cars to the sale (these need to be removed after the sale, but save for the next one). You can look for trash treasures during the week, revamp them with paint or whatever, and sell them at your sale or if you live on a busy street, simply put them out with a price sign. Have a little sign, possibly, "Susie's Saturday Sale" or "Ann's Attic Treasures" out on the days you are selling. One word of advice: To keep your neighbors happy, have one of the older kids keep cars from parking on other people's grass, etc. Also, keep a low profile. You do not want people in your neighborhood to think you have a real business. Having one per month should give you enough time to revamp lots of stuff you hoard and keep the neighbors happy. If you do not have a garage, use your imagination. Do you have an extra room to store and revamp your stuff or even to sell it in there like a little shop? What about cleaning out the shed and making a really cute little house to sell in? Having an Eternal Yard Sale can be highly profitable, and it is fun to do.

6. Business in a Box: See the set-up on page 175.

7. Landscaping yards. You probably have all it takes to do a yard. Gardeners love this job and it gives you a chance to work outside.

8. Painting. We absolutely hate to paint, but homemakers can paint a room and save someone big bucks over the professional painter. Place that ad!

9. Pass out flyers to every office you see and advertise your ability to use a computer. You will be surprised how many office managers need help with data processing from your home!

10. Cleaning offices is hard, but easier than cleaning houses. Place an ad for this one and get going. You probably already have everything at home that you need to do this business!

11. Have a car? Hate being in an office all day? Deliver everything from pizza to flowers to groceries.

12. Call real estate agents and ask them to call you the next time they need a house cleaned.

13. Be brave. Open your own consignment shop or junk shop. Go "trash pickin'" for treasures you can revamp.

Business in a Box

Don't work outside the home, but would like some extra money? Our neatest idea yet for you . . . A "Business in a Box!" We've found that potpourri sells the best with candy fairly close to it. You can do this anytime of day . . . whatever hour you want. It is cash money and is earned instantly! It's not for everyone, but it beats working for someone else at $5.00 an hour . . . we have EASILY made $20 to $40 per hour!!! The plan? Go to any safe neighborhood, knock on the door, and ask if they would be interested in buying a bag of potpourri from you to help with your family expenses. We can count on one hand the times we've been told no! You will find that people think the potpourri or candy bags are cute and most people want to buy—they appreciate you trying to help your family. You can easily make as much money in one day or two than in a week of work somewhere else. Also, you are your own boss and can bag the potpourri while you relax at home watching TV. (Hint: The rich people love the look of the bags for their dinner parties as do real estate people at open houses.) Some cities do require a peddler's license, so check. Once you do this, you will be shocked at how easy and fast this business is!

Costs: A cardboard box, SILK ribbon of the $1/2$ inch size, a box of baggies (the fold over type, generic brand), the $1.00 bag of potpourri at a dollar store (this will make 8 to 10 little baggies), little tags (you can make these from wallpaper books or old cards), a hole puncher, a pair of scissors and 10 one-dollar bills for change. Make your ribbons and/or tags reflect the holidays as well as just colorful for any occasion.

You will also need a basket to carry them in: We sometimes put in a red bandanna in the bottom for the Fourth of July, a paper doily for a more elegant effect, or a swag of Christmas material, plus many more touches. Be creative! But remember, how you look yourself as well as the presentation of your basket will both affect your success.

THIS IS YOUR BOX (view from above looking down)

potpourri bag	ribbon box (ribbons cut about 10" long)
potpourri bag	hole puncher and old cards, wallpaper sheets, gift tags, pair of scissors
Put another smaller box here to empty your potpourri bags so you can grab a full bag.	grocery-type bag to hold finished baggies
	fold-top baggies

NOTE: I take my Business in a Box when I go to the doctor or have to wait for my children, ballgames, etc. You'll be amazed at how many you can make.

P.S. Your profit on the dollar should be about 85 to 90 cents!

New Best Buys for the Tightwad Shopper

We always say "Never buy new when used will do," but if you must, then here is our recommended list of new best buys. Over the years we've received a lot of feedback from our readers concerning the products that they buy. Here's a list of what we personally judge are the best buys for you. Remember, this is only our opinion, combining all information available to us through many resources. By the way, Susan is the "used" one.

BEST CARBON-MONOXIDE DETECTORS:
Nighthawk 2000

BEST VACUUM CLEANERS:
Hoover Power Drive Supreme

BEST SMOKE DETECTORS:
First Alert Double System

BEST LOW-FLOW TOILETS:
Gerber Ultra Flush

BEST LOW-FLOW SHOWERHEADS:
Teledyne Water Pik Original Shower Massage

BEST ELECTRIC BLANKETS:
J.C. Penny Odyssey

BEST AIR CONDITIONERS:
Carrier

BEST WASHING MACHINE REPAIR HISTORY:
(FEWEST REPAIRS)
KitchenAid

BEST CLOTHES DRYER REPAIR HISTORY:
We have found that KitchenAid, Whirlpool, Maytag and Sears
need fewer repairs.

BEST MICROWAVE OVENS:
Samsung

PART FOUR

THE SILVER LINING: Testimonials That Say These Tips Really Work!

The Silver Lining

Okay, okay . . . this is the last section in the book. Ann wrote the introductions so I, Susan, am writing the last one. By now, you may think that our advice is either fabulous or food for hogs; however, you may change your mind after this chapter of true success stories. These people stepped up to the tightwad plate and made their lives better and easier. This chapter was written solely to help you through any financial hardship you may be going through. There's hope for your plight! We have called this chapter "The Silver Lining" because it is sometimes difficult to see the silver lining in those BILLowing clouds that loom over us in life. Everyone needs a bit of motivation. We hope you are truly inspired by the many financial situations you will read about in the following letters from our precious tightwad readers: It's their gift to you! But first, a photo of us with our strollers. Remember when we said to not be discouraged, do what is best for you, and don't be afraid to try something new? Well, here is Ann (on the left) who is wearing an Annie Oakley sweater. She drove me nuts because she was really convinced that Annie Oakley was named after her AND SHE EVEN SLEPT IN THAT SWEATER! Talk about needing a reality check . . . . cccchhheeezzzz!

Let's get on with the letters . . .

"Dear twins, I cannot tell you much you have changed my life with the Business in a Box plan and also the Susie's Saturday Sale idea. I heard you speak on the radio and went to your Web site to see what you two are all

about. I really did not want to go to an outside job after my kids were in school. So a friend and I walked off over forty pounds EACH selling our craft items door to door making cash money that very day. Sometimes we made over $50.00 in only two hours. We chose safe neighborhoods like you said and made our crafts at night in our individual homes after the family was settled for the evening. Occasionally we took a day together during the day to make them and then sold them the other days. My sister actually had a garage sale at least once a month and followed twin Susan's plan. Her name is Elaine and she called her sale "Elaine's Eternal Yard Sale." She followed your rules faithfully and the neighbors did not even notice. I can tell that you two stand by what you preach and I am thankful. Ignore the people who do not understand your tightwad ways. You guys really help people. Keep on truckin', twins!"

— DIANE V., TAMPA, FLORIDA

We were doing a radio show and the audience called in questions or comments. Here is a true story of a man who warmed our hearts:

"Twins, I just had to call in and tell you how you saved my life financially. I am a divorced man that has to pay child support for my two girls. I just could not make ends meet. Your daddy's idea about the Boards and Block kitchen really saved me! I was renting a room with a private bath from a good friend of mine who has a family. It was awkward every time I had to go to the kitchen for a

snack or even to come in and out of the house. I felt like I was intruding. So, I asked him if we could put the rather tall window in my bedroom on a long piano-type hinge so that it opened outward and he agreed. We then built a simple removable hall partition to section my bedroom and bath off from the rest of the house. Now, here is the part that saved me. We put together a simple countertop board on concrete blocks and I bought a tiny refrigerator, microwave, toaster, and hot plate and put it right next to the bathroom near running water so I could wash my dishes there. It is perfect. I even made a little patio area right outside my new-found 'door.' We all have privacy and I am living cheaply and also helping my friend with his mortgage payment! So, I guess he is 'making money while he sleeps!'"

—Richard B., St. Louis, Missouri

"Susan and Ann, I am writing to thank you for your books. They have helped me so much. I was able to finally quit my job this year because of many of your tips PLUS I took the second income test that I heard about when you were on radio one Saturday morning. I could not wait to tell my husband when he got home about the test results! I was not only working for no profit, but I was in the hole more than $100 per month! I gave my notice on Monday and, although it was a little scary, we shaved the working expenses from the budget and we have never regretted it. Now I am addicted to saving even more money. We are trying to find just the right person to rent out a

bedroom and a bath we have cleaned out because we bunked our two boys together in one room. They love being together and when they hate being together as teenagers (we have a few more years) we will be ahead on our mortgage payment for all of those years. It is such a simple idea. I wonder why we did not think of it earlier? I cannot imagine having a free mortgage payment each month. Thanks so much for remembering the everyday person on a budget . . . I truly felt like the "forgotten woman" you spoke about.

—PAM S., AUSTIN, TEXAS

"Dear little twins, thanks to your books, I have color-coded my house, my children and my husband. The dog is next! We no longer yell and scream at each other trying to get out the door in the mornings. We are all packed up the night before and no one eats an evening snack until they are organized for the next day. The kids pick out their outfits for the next week all at one time and we hang those complete outfits on the masking tape that says "Monday, Tuesday, etc." No changing their minds. I warned them so there is no fighting in the morning or every night as to what they are going to wear! I even saved the plastic rings from the milk jugs and looped it over the hanger to add another hanger from another hanger. My husband thought I was flipping when he saw this tip, but he marveled at how well it worked. We also tried the plastic six-pack rings, and socks hang great on those and over a hanger. We have ONE laundry station *now, ONE calendar, ONE day to clean, and it goes on and on. It is so simple once you get organized! Even my trunk is clean and organized with a box for each child. I feel like I have my life back and can rest a bit on my days off and not be such a nag. I called a family meeting like you said and, after I had planned what I wanted the home to be like "organized," I laid it out. I showed everyone where the laundry would be gathered every day during the "five-minutes-before-you-go-to-bed-pick-up," I showed them the table setting items . . . the paper ones for snacks, the school bag place and lunch box place in the refrigerator . . . you name it . . . I covered it. That day I became the CEO of running my home. I am so glad you mentioned those words on radio. It opened my eyes and I bought all of your books online. Please continue helping women who are rushed for time and low on money. I appreciate you two!"*

—SANDY T., SEATTLE, WASHINGTON

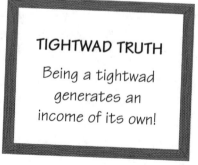

TIGHTWAD TRUTH

Being a tightwad
generates an
income of its own!

We could go on and on with examples of men and women who actually put the tips to work and changed their life financially, but there is not enough space in this book to put them all! We get e-mails every day like this. These letters truly touch us.

It's here where we both remind you of our mission way back in chapter one. That is to help you realize financial freedom through money-saving tips, cash-making ideas, cost-cutting bill-slashers, and, most of all, financial tips that can change your life today. We hope we have done that. Our financial plans are not for everyone, as we have spoken many, many times to people throughout our tightwad trip here on earth. However, if we have helped even one person financially or time-wise, then we are grateful. We also remind you of our target . . . the forgotten woman or family who is really struggling daily. We leave you with these final tightwad thoughts:

- To be successful with our tightwad tips and plans, you must FIRST actually DO them!
- Plan your work and work your plan.
- Don't let others discourage you from helping yourself or your family financially. Do what is best for you! They do not walk in your shoes. REMEMBER, don't be afraid to try something new; amateurs built the Ark, professionals built the *Titanic*!
- Consult with your family and help them realize that a budget plan will set you free financially and is not a prison; rather, the bills and money leaks are your prison!
- Follow our truths, use our common cents, read our motivating success stories, and most of all, do not be discouraged or stressed.

And remember, it's not how much you make, it's how much you get to keep!

One last tightwad tip . . .

. . . for attractive lips, speak kind words.

. . . for lovely eyes, seek out the good in people.

. . . for beautiful hair, let a child run their fingers through it.

. . . for poise, walk with knowledge and with peace.

. . . for courage, remember us . . . we've been where you've been, SURVIVED, and even THRIVED!

Now, Get Going on Your Tightwad Trip to Financial Peace!

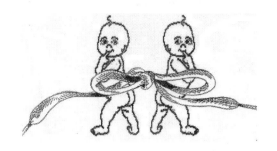

About the Twins

ANN FOX CHODAKOWSKI lives in Brandon, Florida. She holds a master's degree in education and is a retired teacher. A mother of two adult children, Emily and Nathan, she is also a grandmother of three (so far!). She definitely believes she is the smarter twin and can prove it.

SUSAN FOX WOOD lives in the twins' hometown of Paducah, Kentucky. She holds an associate degree as well as many other awards celebrating her gift for organization. She has an adult daughter, Holley, and is a grandmother of one (so far!). She believes that SHE is the smarter twin and that Ann is just plain cheap!

And that's the truth.

You've seen and heard them everywhere . . . .
television, radio, newpapers, and major magazines.
If you'd like to reach them, just go on the Web!
And remember, the twins have three talents:
they are twins, they are tightwads,
and they can really talk!

www.tightwadtwins.com

THE TIGHTWAD TWINS . . .
Saving You Money by the Dumpster-Full!

THE TIGHTWAD END

Experience the Power of Positive Thinking

Change Almost Anything in 21 Days
Expanded Edition
Recharge Your Life with the Power of Over 500 Affirmations

i can do it!

Ruth Fishel
Illustrated by Bonny Van de Kamp

Code 0677 • Paperback • $12.95

Change Almost Anything in 21 Days provides both the inspiration and motivation needed to make important changes—from careers and relationships to parenting and health.

The wisdom this book offers will help you discover how to better understand yourself and find fulfillment by being who you are.

ATTENTION SHOPPERS!

The Woman's Guide to Enlightenment Through Shopping

EVE ELIOT

Code 0995 • Paperback • $10.95

Available wherever books are sold.
To order direct: Phone 800.441.5569 • Online www.hcibooks.com
Prices do not include shipping and handling. Your response code is BKS.